# Cambridge Elements

Elements in the Philosophy of Georg Wilhelm Friedrich Hegel
edited by
Sebastian Stein
*Heidelberg University*
Joshua Wretzel
*Pennsylvania State University*

# HEGEL AND HEIDEGGER ON TIME

Ioannis Trisokkas
*University of Athens*

CAMBRIDGE
UNIVERSITY PRESS

Shaftesbury Road, Cambridge CB2 8EA, United Kingdom

One Liberty Plaza, 20th Floor, New York, NY 10006, USA

477 Williamstown Road, Port Melbourne, VIC 3207, Australia

314–321, 3rd Floor, Plot 3, Splendor Forum, Jasola District Centre, New Delhi – 110025, India

103 Penang Road, #05–06/07, Visioncrest Commercial, Singapore 238467

Cambridge University Press is part of Cambridge University Press & Assessment, a department of the University of Cambridge.

We share the University's mission to contribute to society through the pursuit of education, learning and research at the highest international levels of excellence.

www.cambridge.org
Information on this title: www.cambridge.org/9781009581806

DOI: 10.1017/9781009581837



When citing this work, please include a reference to the DOI 10.1017/9781009581837

First published 2025

*A catalogue record for this publication is available from the British Library*

ISBN 978-1-009-58180-6 Hardback
ISBN 978-1-009-58185-1 Paperback
ISSN 2976-5684 (online)
ISSN 2976-5676 (print)

# Hegel and Heidegger on Time

Elements in the Philosophy of Georg Wilhelm Friedrich Hegel

DOI: 10.1017/9781009581837
First published online: February 2025

Ioannis Trisokkas
*University of Athens*

**Author for correspondence:** Ioannis Trisokkas, idtrisokkas@philosophy.uoa.gr

**Abstract:** This Element discusses Heidegger's early (1924–31) reading and critique of Hegel, which revolve around the topic of time. The standard view is that Heidegger distances himself from Hegel by arguing that whereas he takes time to be 'originarily' Dasein's 'temporality', Hegel has a 'vulgar' conception of time as 'now-time' (the succession of formal nows). The Element defends the thesis that while this difference concerning the nature of time is certainly a part of Heidegger's 'confrontation' with Hegel, it is not its kernel. What Heidegger aspired to convey with his Hegel-critique is that they have a divergent conception of man's understanding of being (ontology). Whereas Heidegger takes ontology as grounded in temporality, Hegel thinks it is grounded in 'the concept', which has a dimension ('logos') manifesting eternity or timelessness. It is argued, contra Kojève, that Heidegger's *reading* (but not necessarily his *critique*) of Hegel is, in an important respect, correct.

This Element also has a video abstract: www.cambridge.org/trisokkas-abstract

**Keywords:** Hegel, Heidegger, time, temporality, ontology



ISBNs: 9781009581806 (HB), 9781009581851 (PB), 9781009581837 (OC)
ISSNs: 2976-5684 (online), 2976-5676 (print)

# Contents

## Introduction

This Element deliberates over Heidegger's early reading and critique of Hegel, a philosopher he considers 'the representative of metaphysics par excellence' (Schmidt 1988: xii). 'Early' refers to Heidegger's philosophical production from 1924, when he writes *The Concept of Time*, to 1930–1, when he composes *Hegel's Phenomenology of Spirit*. The centre of this period is the great but incomplete *Being and Time*, published in 1927.

Early Heidegger 'confronts' Hegel (HPG 44/31, 55/38, 92/65), one of his 'life-long concerns' (Schmidt 1988: 13), on the problematic of *time*. He seeks to differentiate his own view of time's 'originary' (*ursprünglich*) nature, of what time is essentially (BPP 268), from Hegel's. Heidegger argues that while, for him, time is 'originarily' 'temporality', Hegel has a 'vulgar' appreciation of time, regarding it as fundamentally 'now-time', which is a notion standing for the endless succession of nows.

Although this dispute concerning the nature of *time* is an important aspect of Heidegger's early 'confrontation' with Hegel, in this Element I defend the thesis that the quintessential issue in this 'confrontation' is the nature of *the understanding of being* (ontology). Heidegger seeks to convey that while for him ontology is grounded in time (temporality), for Hegel it is grounded in 'the concept', which, Heidegger contends, is *not* identified with time (now-time or otherwise). Alternatively, while for Heidegger 'the question of the meaning of being' is answered in the horizon of time, Hegel answers it in the horizon of 'the concept'. The significance of this for Hegel studies is that Hegelian philosophy, contra popular opinion,[1] is presented as *not* being 'historicist', as *not* making history the one and absolute ground of the understanding of being. If Heidegger is right, it would be incorrect to say that Hegel historicizes ontology.

The discussion develops in three steps, corresponding to this Element's three sections. Section 1 presents (a) what early Heidegger marks as time's 'vulgar' conception and (b) how this differs from his own view, which regards time 'originarily' as 'temporality'. He advances a transcendental–phenomenological argument seeking to prove that 'now-time' is only a 'derivation' from 'temporality'. Because this Element is intended to be of interest to students of both Hegel *and Heidegger*, Heidegger's argument is expounded in some detail. This is also necessary if we are to understand properly Heidegger's reading and critique of Hegel, the subject matter of Section 2.

Section 2, first, presents Heidegger's account of *Hegel*'s notion of time as an instance of the 'vulgar' conception of time and, second, argues that there is

[1] This popular opinion or 'standard view' of Hegelian philosophy is described by Karpinski (2022: 123) and Welchman (2016: 195–196).

a 'deeper' disagreement between them than the one concerning the nature of time. This 'deeper' disagreement concerns the understanding of being (ontology). While Heidegger takes this understanding to be grounded in time, Hegel takes it to be grounded in 'the concept'. Crucially, Heidegger takes Hegel's 'the concept' *not* to be identical with time. This entails that, for Heidegger, Hegelian philosophy, contra the popular view, does not take history, which is characterized fundamentally by time, to be the ground of ontology.

Section 3 considers the objection that Hegel's position is, when all is said and done, not that different from Heidegger's and, therefore, that Heidegger's reading of Hegel is mistaken. I begin by examining two claims supporting this objection. First, I peruse the thesis that, for Hegel, time covers the same domain as 'the concept'. Second, I assess the contention that, for Hegel, time has a higher status than 'the concept' by being a 'ground' or an 'origin' of it. If any of these two claims held, Hegel, *like Heidegger*, would make time the ground of ontology. I argue that both of these claims fail and, therefore, that Heidegger's reading of Hegel is correct: Hegel does not make time and hence history the ground of ontology. Finally, I discuss a real example of the first claim, namely Alexandre Kojève's hugely influential argument for the thesis that Hegel identifies 'the concept' with time, and demonstrate that it is unsound.

In general, the main task of the Element is to present and elucidate early Heidegger's reading and critique of Hegel. Moreover, it aims at defending Heidegger's conclusion that Hegel does *not* temporalize and hence historicize ontology. It should be emphasized, though, that in this Element *no attempt* is made to *critically examine* Heidegger's *critique* of Hegel and determine whether it is successful or unsuccessful. This is a research question I must pursue in another work.

# 1 Heidegger on Time

## 1.1 Introduction

### *1.1.1 The Question of the Meaning of Being*

*Being and Time*'s penultimate section (§82) is devoted to a discussion of Hegel. Heidegger shows interest in Hegel because Hegel is widely considered a philosopher who regards the understanding of being as 'historical' and hence 'temporal' in character, a thesis held also by Heidegger (SZ 428/480).[2]

[2] For Heidegger, Dasein is historical *because* it is temporal: 'The analysis of the historicality of Dasein aims to show that this entity is not "temporal" because it "stands in history", but rather the opposite, that it does and can exist historically only because it is temporal in the ground of its being' (SZ 376/428, translation modified).

It may thus be thought that Heidegger's painstaking enquiry into the meaning of being led him, when all is said and done, no farther than Hegel.[3]

Heidegger aims at showing that the alleged similarity between his position and Hegel's is deceptive. One way in which he registers this is by arguing that Hegel understands 'time' differently than he does. While Heidegger takes time to be 'originarily' 'temporality' (BPP 241), Hegel, Heidegger contends, takes time to be essentially 'now-time', thus conceiving it in a 'vulgar' (*vulgär*) way (SZ 428/480). This difference concerning time's 'originary constitution' or 'originary structure' (BPP 230) differentiates fundamentally, one may argue, Heidegger's position from Hegel's: while they both affirm that the understanding of being is 'historical' and hence 'temporal', they mean by that entirely different things.

This would seem to establish that the focal point of difference between Heidegger and Hegel is that they have conflicting views on the nature of time. Yet Heidegger's 'confrontation' with Hegel goes deeper than this. *My thesis is that their dispute is not only about the nature of time but also about whether the ground of the understanding of being is time (Heidegger) or 'the concept' (Hegel).*

First, though, I must present *early Heidegger*'s account of time, for his reading and critique *of Hegel* cannot be comprehended without a prior knowledge of *Heidegger*'s theory of time. For this presentation, I will focus on three texts: (a) Division II of *Being and Time* (1927); (b) Part Two of *The Basic Problems of Phenomenology* (hereafter *Basic Problems*), a lecture course delivered in 1927 and described as 'the designed and designated sequel' of *Being and Time* (Hofstadter 1982: xi); and (c) the short piece *The Concept of Time* (1924).

For early Heidegger, philosophy's central question is the question of the meaning (*Sinn*) of being (*Sein*). This question asks 'how does being have a meaning?' or 'how is being understood?' Heidegger writes that time is the 'horizon of any understanding of being at all' (SZ 1/19, 17/39). This means that being is understood through time.[4] Saying this is the same as saying that time is the meaning of being.[5]

---

[3] As Gadamer (1977: 69, 230) reports, Heidegger was frequently criticized that his philosophy is not essentially different from Hegel's. Nikolai Hartmann, Heidegger's colleague in Marburg, had such a view (Williams 1989: 135–136).

[4] Blattner (1999: 2) writes that time's characterization as the 'horizon' of 'any understanding of being at all' means that 'being is to be interpreted or understood in terms of time'. Later he writes that this means 'that ontological frameworks are essentially shot through with temporal elements' (Blattner 1999: 24). Caputo (1977: 91) takes the term 'horizon' to refer to 'the right framework of conditions' and so Heidegger's project to argue for time being the right framework of conditions for any understanding of being at all. Note that the 'understanding of being' here does not refer only or even mainly to a conscious, theoretical ontology, as, for Heidegger, Dasein's understanding of being is mostly pre-theoretical, preconscious, implicit (SZ 12/32, 336/385; Caputo 1986: 123).

[5] Gorner (2007: 153–154) writes that, for Heidegger, 'time is the sense or meaning (*Sinn*) of being' and that 'by *Sinn* Heidegger understands that on the basis of which, or by reference to which, something is understood'.

Heidegger, though, distinguishes between various modes of time (CT 7) and takes *one* of these, 'temporality', to be 'originary'. All other modes 'derive' from – that is, are made possible by – temporality and are, therefore, 'derivative' (BPP 268, 325). Some modes are 'closer' to temporality than others. The mode of time that is the farthest away from temporality is 'now-time', time's 'vulgar' conception (BPP 263).

### *1.1.2 Temporality and Dasein*

It is pivotal to notice from the outset that Heidegger links the enquiry into the meaning of being – that is, the enquiry into 'the understanding of being', namely 'ontology' (with which 'philosophy' is identified) with the understanding of *the being of 'Dasein' or man.*[6] This move is justified via the mediating claim that the understanding of being 'belongs' to Dasein's being (BPP 318). As he puts it in *Basic Problems*, 'to comprehend the understanding of being means first and foremost to understand that being to whose ontological constitution the understanding of being belongs, the Dasein' (BPP 227). Division I of *Being and Time* has as its theme 'the existential analytic of Dasein', which discloses Dasein's 'ontological constitution' or 'basic structures' (BPP 227–228). Division II argues for the thesis that this 'constitution' 'is grounded in temporality' (BPP 228). But what *is* 'temporality'?

The proper way to answer this question, in Heidegger's view, is to begin with the vulgar conception of time and show that it 'presupposes temporality' (BPP 228). This will allow us to see 'that and how' time's vulgar conception 'belongs to and springs from temporality' and will also reveal 'the phenomenon of temporality itself and its basic structure' (BPP 228, 257).

Crucially, Heidegger adds that the move from the vulgar conception of time to its presupposition, temporality, will give us '*insight into the original constitution of the Dasein's being*' (BPP 228). This suggests that temporality is a structure *of* Dasein's being.[7] This must be held in mind when sentences such as this are encountered: '*The ontological condition of the possibility of the understanding of being is temporality itself*' (BPP 228). Temporality is what 'makes ontology possible', 'the horizon from which we understand being' (BPP 228; see also BPP 260), but it is *not* independent of Dasein; it *is* rather 'the original constitution of the Dasein's being', 'what . . . existence . . . proves to be' (BPP 228).

[6] 'The *concept of philosophy* . . . can be expounded only by way of a properly understood concept of the Dasein' (BPP 320).

[7] 'Temporality constitutes the basic constitution of the being we call the Dasein' (BPP 318; see also BPP 325).

## 1.2 Now-Time: The Vulgar Conception of Time

It has been made clear that 'the aim now is to press forward through the vulgar understanding of time toward temporality, in which the Dasein's ontological constitution is rooted and to which time as vulgarly understood belongs' (BPP 229, translation modified). In the realm of 'everyday, circumspective concern' (SZ 420/472),[8] from which phenomenological enquiry always begins, time is 'explicitly' (*ausdrücklich*) conceived as 'now-time' (SZ 420/472–473; BPP 241, 268). Heidegger calls it 'the vulgar conception of time'.[9] In everydayness, time's 'vulgar' conception is the dominant conception and is held and imposed on Dasein by 'the one' (*das Man*) (CT 9, 17). It is espoused by 'traditional' philosophy,[10] which has followed 'the one' on this issue (BPP 257).[11] Aristotle's theory of time lays out 'the essentials' of the vulgar conception (BPP 231; SZ 421/473).[12] Heidegger's thesis is that now-time is a derivative phenomenon: it derives from more 'originary' modes of time, which are *implicitly* at work in everydayness.

The essence of now-time is that it prioritizes the 'now' over the 'before' and the 'after', the 'earlier' and the 'later', the 'at-the-time' and the 'then'.[13] This gives rise to a variety of characterizations of now-time.

*First*, now-time is a 'sequence' or 'succession' of nows (BPP 256; SZ 424/476). As Heidegger puts it, 'for the vulgar understanding of time, time shows itself as a sequence of nows which are constantly "present-at-hand" ("*vorhandenen*"), simultaneously passing-away (*vergehenden*) and coming-to-be (*ankommenden*)' (SZ 422/474, translation modified).[14] The vulgar understanding of time treats time simply as the 'present-at-hand' or 'extant'[15] nows that are

---

8 'Circumspection' is the way in which Dasein pursues its everyday tasks by using equipment.

9 'The factical Dasein experiences and knows time first and primarily only as it is vulgarly understood' (BPP 268, translation modified).

10 'The vulgar understanding of time very early reached conceptual expression in philosophy' (BPP 230). Heidegger speaks frequently of 'the traditional concept of time'; see, for example, BPP 231–232.

11 'On average, the interpretation of Dasein is governed by everydayness, by what one traditionally says about Dasein and human life. It is governed by the "One", by tradition' (CT 9).

12 Aristotle's understanding of time fits the 'natural experience and understanding' of time and came to be identified with it (BPP 229, 255; SZ 421/473). Heidegger writes that 'time as Aristotle expounds it [is time] as it is familiar to ordinary consciousness' (BPP 260) and that now-time is the 'conception of time . . . we grew up with' (Logik 258/214). 'Natural' time, not 'temporality', is, for Aristotle, time's 'originary' being. (Besides understanding 'natural time' as *ordinary* time, Heidegger often explicates 'natural time' as a dimension of *nature* (CT 17, 21)). Given that the Aristotelian conception adopted time's 'vulgar' conception from 'the one', Heidegger claims that Aristotle did not investigate 'the source of the time which is thus manifest' (SZ 421/473).

13 Heidegger makes subtle distinctions between these pairs of 'temporal determinations' (SZ 421/473; BPP 246–247; Blattner 1999: 128–129).

14 'This time of the present is explicated as a sequence constantly rolling through the now' (CT 18).

15 'The nows . . . come and go like beings; like extant entities they perish, becoming no longer extant' (BPP 272).

after-one-another (*Nacheinander*), what is called 'the flow of time' (*der Fluß der Zeit*) or 'the course of time' (*der Lauf der Zeit*) (SZ 422/474; BPP 234). Each now follows a previous now and leads to a new now. Both the succeeded now and the forthcoming now are 'non-existent', 'have the character of a nullity', although they are 'the parts that go to make [time] up' (BPP 233). The former is deemed to be a no-longer-now and the latter a not-yet-now. Given that *each now* succeeds a no-longer-now and will be succeeded by a not-yet-now, the sequence of nows is without beginning and end, 'is endless "on both sides"' (SZ 424/476), and never cancels out the now (SZ 423/475). It is 'infinite' or 'eternal' (SZ 423). As Heidegger has it, 'the sequence of nows is designated as infinite. It is taken to be a universal law that time is infinite' (BPP 260, 273). The now is termed 'the present', the no-longer-now 'the past', and the not-yet-now 'the future'. Out of all these moments, only the now, the present, *is* (BPP 233, 246–247). It is that which 'holds time together with itself as a whole' (BPP 236, 256).

*Second*, the now is purified: it is not *itself* empirical. Heidegger speaks of 'naked' and 'pure' nows (BPP 259, 271). The now is merely a formal 'container' 'filled' with empirical content (BPP 252). This is why Dasein and the other entities are said to be '*in* time' (BPP 234, 254; CT 3–4).

*Third*, now-time is 'a unidirectional irreversible sequence of nows one after the other' (BPP 257). Precisely because the succession is irreversible, the past is 'irretrievable' (CT 18). Heidegger relates the past's irretrievability with an erroneous view of history. This view distinguishes sharply between (a) a past that is 'closed off' from the present, merely 'what was going on', and (b) the present as what is 'other' than the past (CT 19). For this view, history is identified with (a).

*Fourth*, now-time 'reveals itself in counting' (SZ 421/473, translation modified; see also BPP 235, 254, 257) and so exhibits a numerical structure (BPP 256, 261) or has the form of measurement (CT 3). Being numerical, now-time abstracts from any content. As Heidegger phrases it, 'time as number . . . does not itself belong to the entity that it counts' (BPP 250).[16] Since (a) time is traditionally considered one of nature's fundamental dimensions (the other being space) and (b) time is numerical, the vulgar conception of time is one of the pillars of the mathematization of nature (CT 4).

[16] Heidegger stresses that now-time's counting character belongs to Dasein, the being that counts (BPP 239). But this is a feature *he* ascribes to now-time rather than an 'essential determination' of it that the vulgar conception itself explicitly ascribes to it. He writes, for example, that Aristotle does not pursue the question 'whether, if there is no soul, time does or does not exist' 'any further' (BPP 254).

*Fifth*, now-time is 'something connected with motion' (BPP 243; CT 3) or rest, 'a limiting case of motion' (BPP 236). That is, now-time relates to entities that are either in motion or at rest, namely *natural* entities. It does not relate to elements being *beyond motion and rest*, viz. *pure* elements. A triangle is 'beyond rest and motion' and, therefore, is not 'embraced' by time (BPP 253). Time 'embraces or *holds around* the moving and resting things' (BPP 252). It is a 'container', 'the formal element of holding-around' natural or empirical things (BPP 252).

*Sixth*, by being numerical, now-time is *spatialized*. Numbers do belong to an arithmetical sequence, but one is not 'earlier' or 'later' than another. This is why numbers can be used to measure a *spatial* area. By attributing a numerical structure to time, the vulgar conception 'assimilates' time to space. Because each number exemplifies a collection of 'homogeneous' units (the units of space), time is, through number, 'homogenized' (CT 18). Time's 'homogenization' is what underlies the sequence of nows' being an 'infinity' of equal, uniform, naked nows (CT 4).

## 1.3 The Use of the Clock and Time-Reckoning

In everydayness, now-time is 'shown' to Dasein by means of a specific equipment (BPP 258), the clock (in any of its forms: the 'pocket watch' (SZ 416), 'the shadow' (SZ 421), 'the sun' (BPP 240; CT 5)). Dasein 'reads' now-time 'off' the use of the clock (BPP 240).[17] The use of the clock, that is, presents time as a sequence of nows, purified from empirical content, irreversible, a numerical structure, what formally embraces natural things, and a homogenized, spatialized element. This is how time appears *explicitly*, as a *thematic* phenomenon characterized by *presence-at-hand*, 'a merely extant thing' (BPP 259).[18] 'The one' 'directs' itself 'naturally' to time through the use of the clock (SZ 420/473; BPP 257).

The clock manifests time as *now*-time because it works through the travelling pointer (BPP 240). This brings Dasein's attention constantly to the now[19] and turns the past into what is no longer shown by the pointer and the future into what is not yet shown by it (CT 4, 17). All 'occurrences . . . are encountered as running through a present' (CT 18). Moreover, the particular 'shape' of the

[17] Heidegger distinguishes reading 'off' the clock, which he consigns to time's vulgar conception, from reading 'from' the clock, which he associates with time-reckoning and significance (BPP 261–262). He evidently thinks that not only traditional philosophy but also science reads time off the clock (CT 2–3).

[18] 'The vulgar understanding of time manifests itself explicitly and primarily in the use of the clock' (BPP 257, translation modified). See also BPP 260, 271–272.

[19] 'What primarily the clock does in each case is . . . to determine the specific fixing of the now. If I take out my watch, then the first thing I say is: "Now it is nine o'clock"' (CT5).

pointer's endless movement manifests time as a succession of 'identical' ('homogenized') nows which 'reveal themselves in counting' and hence are numbers (SZ 420/473; CT 4). Finally, the *single* direction of the pointer's movement establishes the past's irretrievability. This last point goes together with Dasein's 'busyness' in its everydayness, where Dasein is so 'busy' that it 'clings to its present' and 'fails to see what is past' (CT 19).

Heidegger argues that the use of the clock, counting on the basis of the moving pointer, which is now-time's origin, 'derives' from (i.e. is made possible by) a certain mode of time he calls 'time-reckoning' (BPP 258).[20] The question is *why* Dasein uses the clock (*why* does it count the nows?).[21] Heidegger's response is that it does this so as to *reckon with time*. Time-reckoning is Dasein's 'use of time' so as to *estimate* and *order* its actions and tasks: it determines which action/task comes before or earlier than another, which after or later than another, and which now, and also how much time each will take, so as to press ahead in its projections (the 'in-order-to') and self-understanding.[22] The clock is simply the tool Dasein employs to estimate and order its scheduled tasks *in a precise, efficient way*.[23] Time-reckoning (the use of time) is prior to the use of the clock (measurement).[24] As Heidegger writes, 'we measure time *because* we need and use time, *because* we take time or let it pass, and explicitly regulate and make secure the way we use time by specific time measurement' (BPP 260, my emphasis).

The use of the clock makes thematic or explicit (and thereby 'modifies') what is unthematic or implicit in time-reckoning. In time-reckoning we 'are abandoned to' time 'as to the most commonplace thing, whether we are lost in it or pressed by it' (BPP 229). The counting of time makes explicit our temporal estimation and ordering. As Heidegger puts it, 'the "more naturally" the concern

---

[20] Heidegger distinguishes between time-reckoning and the use of the clock on BPP 229: 'We constantly reckon with time or take account of it without explicitly measuring it by the clock.' He asks what 'makes' the use of the clock 'itself possible' (BPP 257). Time-reckoning is 'the original mode of being' of this use (BPP 258).

[21] This is how I understand Heidegger's question 'What does it mean to speak of using a clock?' (BPP 257).

[22] This is why Heidegger writes that 'the nows [of the clock] can be expressed and understood only in the horizon of the earlier and later' (BPP 246). He gives this example of time-reckoning: 'In noting the time, I am trying to determine what time it is, how much time there is till nine o'clock, so as to finish this or that subject. In ascertaining the time, I am trying to find out how much time there is *till this or that point* so that I may see that I have enough time, so much time, *in order* to finish the subject' (BPP 258).

[23] 'It is on the basis of this original comportment toward time that we arrive at the measuring of time, that we invent clocks in order to shape our reckoning with time more economically with reference to time' (BPP 258).

[24] 'We are always already reckoning with time, taking it into account, before we look at a clock to measure the time' (BPP 258). See also CT 14: 'the original way of dealing with time is not a measuring'.

which gives itself time reckons with time, the less it dwells at the expressed time (*ausgesprochenen Zeit*) as such; rather it is lost in the equipment with which it is concerned, which in each case has its own time' (SZ 422/474). In everydayness, Dasein reckons with time, but this happens unthematically, in the manner of the equipment's readiness-to-hand (*Zuhandenheit*). When time-reckoning is turned into now-time through the use of the clock, time appears 'explicitly' or 'expressly' as presence-at-hand (*Vorhandenheit*). This transformation goes hand in hand with Dasein's *reading now-time off the use of the clock*.

The question is *why* Dasein reckons with time. This leads to time-reckoning's 'derivation' from another structure of time.

## 1.4 World-Time

Dasein reckons with time because its worldly existence is determined by a mode of time called 'world-time'. World-time has four defining features: datability, spannedness, significance, and publicness (SZ 416/469; BPP 261–264). Let me describe each in turn.

### *(a)* Datability *(*Datierbarkeit*)*

World-time is datable in the sense that the now (but also the earlier and the later) is always a 'now when' (as in 'now when I am playing the piano') (SZ 407/459; BPP 262). Each temporal moment hooks to an *event* and is *never* devoid of the content this event gives it; it is never 'naked', 'free-floating', and 'relationless' (BPP 263). The use of the clock comes after datability. In world-time, Dasein understands what it does without first assigning clock-time to it. 'Now, at 16:15, when I am playing the piano' comes after 'now when I am playing the piano' and only when the datable now becomes 'present-at-hand' or 'thematic'.

### *(b)* Spannedness *(*Gespanntheit*)*

World-time is spanned in the sense that the now (and the earlier and the later) is never instantaneous or 'punctualized' (BPP 264, 270); it always lasts for a 'stretch' (BPP 263, 269–270). When we say 'now when I am playing the piano', we refer to an act that began in the past, is materialized now, and will continue in the future (SZ 409/462). It 'stretches out' (BPP 263). This 'stretch's' specific duration, whether it is one hour or two, is determined only afterwards (BPP 248–249, 263).

### *(c)* Significance *(*Bedeutsamkeit*)*

World-time is significant in the sense that each now (and earlier and later) is deemed right/appropriate or wrong/inappropriate time (SZ 414/467;

BPP 261, 271). Time's rightness or wrongness relates to whether it is the right or the wrong time *to perform an event* within 'the world' (BPP 261). If now I am watching a movie instead of reading for tomorrow's history test, as I should be doing, I deem this the wrong time to be watching a movie.

### *(d)* Publicness *(Öffentlichkeit)*

World-time is public in that every now (and earlier and later) is shared and expressed by all Dasein (SZ 411/463–464), 'the one' (*das Man*) (CT 17). So Dasein's dated nows can be understood and experienced by other Dasein. Heidegger makes this point as follows:

> As we express the dated and spanned now *in our being with one another*, each one of us understands the others. When any one of us says 'now', we all understand this now, even though each of us perhaps dates this now by starting from a different thing or event. . . . The expressed now is intelligible to everyone in our being with one another. Although each one of us utters his own now, it is nevertheless the now for everyone. The accessibility of the now for everyone, without prejudice to the diverse datings, characterizes time as public. (BPP 264)

How does world-time ground time-reckoning? Dasein reckons with time *only because* its existence is temporally determined by nows that are dated, spanned, significant, and public. Dasein exists by caring for itself and other entities. Its care occurs by projecting and undertaking tasks and pressing towards them by performing actions and using equipment and interacting with other Dasein in a common world. All these are temporally determined. It is *now* that Dasein exists in such a way. Yet this now is not the now of now-time, for it is hooked to an event. This differentiates the successive nows of Dasein's existence qualitatively. Now when-I-am-playing-the-piano is qualitatively distinct from now-when-I-am-studying-for-the-history-test. Moreover, these nows are not instantaneous: all last for a 'stretch', which is usually different for each. Additionally, there is a right and a wrong time to undertake certain actions and project certain tasks. I should not be playing the piano when it is the wrong time to do it – that is, when I should be studying for the history test. Finally, Dasein's actions and tasks are embedded in a public network of significance. Not only do other Dasein have access to Dasein's actions and tasks, but also the other Dasein's actions and tasks affect Dasein's behaviour. If my history teacher had not decided that pupils will take a test tomorrow, I would not now be studying for the test instead of playing the piano and would not be planning what to do from now till tomorrow the exact way I do.

*Because* the now of my existence is a world-time now, I reckon with time. I estimate the duration of the actions pertaining to my tasks and order them *because* I cannot do all I am supposed to do at once and actions/tasks must be connected in a certain way. Actions are different from one another, last differently, and lead to or presuppose one another, so I cannot but undertake them successively and estimate their duration accurately if I want to press towards my tasks and self-understanding. *Since* there is a right and a wrong time to do things, in terms of both what I have decided and what public Dasein has decided, I must estimate the duration of my actions and order them in a certain way. This is exactly what reckoning with time means. So Dasein reckons with time *because* the nows determining its existence are dated, spanned, significant, and public, not the other way around.[25]

## 1.5 Temporality

Time-reckoning 'derives' from world-time, but world-time 'derives' from 'temporality'.[26] Temporality consists of the unity of (a) 'retaining', (b) 'awaiting' (or 'expecting') and (c) 'enpresenting' (BPP 269). I will first describe each of these 'moments', which are 'comportments' of Dasein (BPP 257), and then explain how this unity, which is 'ecstatic' in character, an 'openness', grounds world-time.[27]

### *(a)* Retaining *(*Behalten*)*

Retaining is the temporal determination of Dasein's *being-already* and what 'earlier'/'before'/'at-the-time' 'originarily' means (rather than no-longer-now) (BPP 259, 261, 263, 265). It denotes the 'erstwhile' context *from* which an event is launched (BPP 245, 259). It signifies that the world into which Dasein has been thrown has already made things available to it as things *mattering* to it (CT 9). Dasein's retaining involves also its having already found the equipment of its wherewithal *reliable* and its having already had the *ability* to use it.

---

25 'The time with which we reckon … is datable, spanned, public, and has the character of significance, belonging to the world itself' (BPP 264).

26 Heidegger asks: 'But how do these structural moments [of world-time] belong essentially to time? How are these structures themselves possible?' (BPP 264). He answers: '*These structures* must *become ontologically intelligible by way of the ecstatic-horizonal constitution of temporality*' (BPP 268).

27 That Heidegger attempts to ground world-time in retaining-awaiting-enpresenting is suggested by the following: 'Can these structural moments of time [i.e. datability, spannedness, significance, publicness] … be understood … by means of enpresenting, expecting, and retaining?' (BPP 265). He also writes that 'we can see from the elucidation of the structural moments of significance, datability, spannedness, and publicness that and how the basic determinations of time in the vulgar sense arise from the ecstatic-horizonal unity of expecting, retaining, and enpresenting' (BPP 271).

### *(b)* Awaiting *(*Gewärtigen*)*

Awaiting is the temporal determination of Dasein's *being-ahead* and what 'later'/'after'/'then' 'originarily' means (rather than not-yet-now) (BPP 259, 261, 263). It is the '*to*-there' of an event that is (already) 'from-there' (BPP 245). It signifies that Dasein *projects* tasks and a self-understanding. Awaiting can, although this is not a given,[28] take the form of Dasein's understanding itself as *finite* and projecting an end or a non-being for itself – that is, its *death*. This projection *is* Dasein's '*most extreme possibility of being*' (CT 10) and is activated only in Dasein's *authentic* existence. When this happens, things matter to Dasein from the perspective of its own finitude and not *sub specie aeternitatis*.

### *(c)* Enpresenting *(*Gegenwärtigen*)*

Enpresenting is the temporal determination of Dasein's *being-amidst* and *being-with* and is expressed by 'now' (BPP 261, 263; CT 16). It signifies that Dasein *acts*, that it *actually* takes the equipment *amidst* the wherewithal in a social world (i.e. in a world where Dasein is *with* other Dasein) and *presses ahead* towards the task and the self-understanding it has in mind (BPP 265; CT 16)[29] or, if it exists 'authentically', that it acts while having its non-being in mind.[30]

How does this structure ground world-time? In world-time, each now (and earlier and later) is dated, spanned, significant, and public. Let us take *now-when-I-am-studying-for-the-history-test*. This cannot *be* unless studying for the history test has *already* mattered to me and I have *already* been familiar with an array of equipment which I find reliable. I must have *already* attended school and acquired certain abilities (e.g. reading and writing), the school must have *already* developed a procedure for examinations which I must have *already* been aware of, the teacher must have *already* gotten a degree in history, and so on. *Thus a world-time now depends upon Dasein's retaining.*

---

[28] Dasein's end belongs to it fundamentally, but its *understanding* is *not* there 'at first and for the most part'. Rather, what *is* there 'primarily' is Dasein's looking away from its end (CT 10).

[29] 'And finally, whenever I say "now" I am comporting myself . . . toward something present which is in my present. This comportment toward something present, this having-there of something present, a having which expresses itself in the now, we call the *enpresenting* of something' (BPP 260).

[30] Heidegger clarifies that in authentic existence death does not have a physical presence (an *im*possibility) but rather a presence *in Dasein's mind*:

> The end of my Dasein, my death, is not some point at which a sequence of events suddenly breaks off, but a possibility which Dasein *knows* of in this or that way: the most extreme possibility of itself, which it can seize and appropriate as standing before it. Dasein has *in itself* the possibility of meeting with its death as the most extreme possibility of itself. This most extreme possibility of Being has the character of a standing-before in *certainty*, and this certainty for its part is characterized by an utter indeterminacy. (CT 11, my emphasis)

Moreover, no now-when-I-am-studying-for-the-history-test can *be* unless it associates with a projection of tasks and a self-understanding. I am now studying for the history test because I intend to finish school and go to the university or/and because I conceive of myself as a responsible person who wants to please his parents. I do certain things at a certain time *because* I *project* tasks and *understand myself* in a certain way. *So a world-time now depends upon Dasein's awaiting.*

Finally, no now-when-I-am-studying-for-the-history-test can *be* unless I am actually studying for the history test. Dasein's retaining and awaiting cannot on their own produce this world-time now. There must also be enpresenting, actually grasping the history book, paper, and pencil, and starting reading and taking notes. The now is dated only because there is enpresenting (BPP 269). *So a world-time now depends upon Dasein's enpresenting.*

Retaining-awaiting-enpresenting is a unitary structure (BPP 260–261). Heidegger calls it 'ecstatic unity' (BPP 318) and 'originary unity' (BPP 266, translation modified). There is *not* first retaining, then awaiting, and then enpresenting. They function together, not successively (CT 16): *at every now* I am retaining, awaiting, and enpresenting. This unity disappears in now-time, where enpresenting (looking at the clock's travelling pointer) dominates retaining and awaiting (SZ 421/473–474). *Precisely because* enpresenting takes over in now-time, this 'derivative' temporal mode transforms the 'earlier' (past) and the 'later' (future) into 'no-longer-now' and 'not-yet-now' (SZ 421). Heidegger remarks that for 'the one' time is what is shown in such dominant enpresenting (SZ 421/473–474; CT 16–17). By disregarding the *unity* of retaining-awaiting-enpresenting, the vulgar conception of time apprehends the time-determinations without their 'stretch' or 'spannedness' (BPP 270), turning them thus into instantaneous, disappearing nows. Without this 'stretch' time loses its *historical* nature, for the past ('from-there') becomes something alien and 'irretrievable' (CT 19–20).

Retaining-awaiting-enpresenting is the temporality of Dasein's comportment towards beings (including itself and other Dasein) in the world (BPP 318). This comportment has the character of 'transcendence' (BPP 268) because it is Dasein's reaching *out* to beings (BPP 322–323). Heidegger states that 'transcendence ... is rooted in temporality' (BPP 323). That which makes possible Dasein's *getting out of itself* and *reaching out to beings* (i.e. 'transcendence') is characterized as 'ecstatic'. This is temporality, the retaining-awaiting-enpresenting, which is *Dasein*'s 'originary constitution'. Being 'ecstatic' means *opening oneself* to beings (BPP 318). Temporality, then, is 'intrinsically open', a 'peculiar *openness*' (BPP 267). Let us delve a little bit deeper into this characterization of temporality as 'openness'.

*First*, Dasein *retains* by being *open* to 'what it already has been' (BPP 265). Things already matter to it because it is open to mattering. This openness *is* the *past* as *having-been-ness* (*Gewesenheit*). This clarifies that things already matter to Dasein because it *lets* them matter to it. The 'originary' past, therefore, is Dasein itself. Dasein's having-been-ness means that it cannot get rid of its past, that the past is 'an essential determination of our existence' (BPP 265). Heidegger writes that 'that which we *are* as having been has not gone by, passed away, in the sense in which we say that we could shuffle off our past like a garment' (BPP 265). What is crucial here is that our having-been determines who we *now are*, that *at each now* we are going-back-to-*ourselves* (BPP 266). As Heidegger puts it, '[Dasein] can *be* as having been only as long as it exists. And it is precisely when Dasein no longer is, that it also no longer has been. It has *been* only so long as it is' (BPP 266). *This* past, this having-been-ness that depends upon our being-now, stems precisely from our openness to mattering.

*Second*, Dasein *awaits* by being *open* to what lies ahead and comes towards it, namely its possibilities. Dasein projects tasks and its self-understanding by being open to what 'comes-toward-itself from out of a possibility of itself' (BPP 266). Through such openness, *Dasein itself* is ahead of *itself* and from there *it* comes towards *itself* (BPP 265). *This clarifies that possibilities come from Dasein itself.* A possibility could not be without Dasein being open to it. This makes temporality, the ground of Dasein's existence, 'the origin of possibility itself' (BPP 325).[31] Dasein's openness to what lies ahead is called *future* 'in an original sense' (BPP 265). Heidegger writes that awaiting is 'the *primary concept of the future*' and that this concept 'is the presupposition [of] the vulgar concept of the future in the sense of the not-yet-now' (BPP 265, translation modified).

*Third*, Dasein *enpresents* by being *open* to its immediate environment and the wherewithal given to it. Dasein is actually playing the piano by being open to grasping this equipment and putting it to use. *Even if* there were a piano around and playing the piano mattered to Dasein and it understood (i.e. projected) itself as a musician, Dasein would not *now* be playing the piano unless it was *open* to grasping and using it.[32] Dasein's openness to actual, in-person use of equipment for the achievement of a certain task is the originary present or *praesens*. It has nothing to do with a present-at-hand, 'pure', 'naked' now (BPP 266).

[31] It is this *emphasis* on Dasein itself, its being placed *explicitly* at the centre of time, that is served by the last step of Heidegger's argument. This is reinforced by statements such as this: 'Even if what we are awaiting may be some event, some occurrence, still our own Dasein is always conjointly awaited in the awaiting of the occurrence itself' (BPP 265, translation modified).

[32] 'This character of being a now-when-this-or-that, the relation of datability, is possible only because the now is ecstatically open as a time-determination, having its source in temporality' (BPP 269).

Dasein's openness to what lies ahead, the originary future, can acquire such a character that *authentic* existence is accomplished through it. This character appears when Dasein is open, not only to what lies ahead (in general), but also to its own death (in particular) (BPP 265), which is a mark of non-being. *In such a case, temporality becomes authentic*. When Dasein's existence is grounded in 'authentic temporality' (CT 7), Dasein *recognizes* its own *finitude* and projects a self-understanding shaped by this finitude.

Originary past, present, and future relate to the past, present, and future of the vulgar understanding of time, since the latter are 'derivatives' of the former, but they differ drastically. They are moments of a unity rather than moments of a succession (Gorner 2007: 156). Moreover, they are characterized by finitude, not infinity. Their openness has a beginning and an end, because (a) it belongs to Dasein's constitution and (b) Dasein begins when it is 'thrown' into 'the world' and ends when it dies. In this way, the understanding of being, ontology itself, as well as the understanding of beings, Dasein's comportment towards beings, are 'temporalized', are *not* 'forever and eternal' (BPP 325); they are rather 'historical' or 'epochal'.

The unity of temporality, then, is finite or 'historical' because it is *Dasein*'s originary constitution.[33] It is 'founded on the Dasein's existence' (BPP 319), which is a 'historical existence' (BPP 322). Dasein is thrown into the world and is determined by death, the end of its being. Its openness is defined by its connection with these elements. It is not an infinite openness. Its boundaries are shaped or 'schematized' by the *specific* world into which Dasein has been thrown and the *specific* death (nothingness) that comes to it. Temporality's 'ecstases' are neither free-floating nor formal. They are 'horizons' or 'schemata' determined by the specificities characterizing Dasein's existence.[34] Temporality, therefore, provides a finite direction, that 'direction [to] which its [i.e. Dasein's] existentiell comportment tends' (BPP 321). It is this finitude that the vulgar conception of time misses:

> The vulgar experience of beings has at its disposal no other horizon for understanding being than that of extantness, being at hand. Matters like significance and datability remain a closed book for this way of understanding being. Time becomes the intrinsically free-floating runoff of a sequence of nows. ... Starting from this view, it arrives at the opinion that time is infinite, endless, whereas by its very nature temporality is finite. (BPP 272)

---

[33] Heidegger writes that the stone is not temporal (BPP 271).

[34] 'That toward which each ecstasis is intrinsically *open* in a *specific* way we call the horizon of the ecstasis' (BPP 267, my emphasis). See also CT 6, 8, where Heidegger makes clear that 'the *specificity* of the "I am" is constitutive for Dasein'.

## 1.6 The Cause of the Vulgar Conception of Time

Heidegger has attempted to show that now-time 'derives' from more 'originary' modes of time. He has argued that 'the one' and traditional philosophy and science determine the nature of time by reading it off the clock, whose use 'derives' from time-reckoning, world-time, and, eventually, Dasein's 'ecstatic' temporality. Without these structures, there would be no use of the clock and hence no now-time.

As time mutates from temporality, world-time, and time-reckoning to now-time, it becomes 'abstract'. Such an abstraction engenders the 'covering up' of those originary structures (SZ 422–423/474–475; BPP 322). As now-time, time is severed from Dasein's openness to mattering and the world's network of significance, the actual wherewithal around it, and the possibilities coming to it (including its death). For the vulgar conception, which Heidegger calls an 'illusion' (BPP 266), only the succession of nows is important.

What, though, is the *cause* of this 'illusion'?[35] *Why* does Dasein 'interpret' time vulgarly *rather than 'originarily'*? On the surface, this seems to be so simply because Dasein, upon its being thrown into 'the world', 'falls' into the being of 'the one' or 'common sense'.[36] As Heidegger puts it,

> it is no accident that world-time thus gets . . . covered up by the way time is vulgarly understood. . . . Just *because* the vulgar interpretation of time maintains itself by looking solely in the direction of concernful common sense, and understands solely what 'shows' itself within the common-sense horizon, these [originary] structures must escape it. (SZ 422/474–475)

'The one's' reign, then, and Dasein's 'falling' into it cause originary time's covering up. The question, however, now becomes why '*the one*' interprets time vulgarly rather than originarily. Why does '*the one*' choose to 'explicitly' understand time off the clock rather than 'off' Dasein's temporality?

Heidegger retorts by referring to the *thinking* of *death* or non-being, 'the most extreme possibility of Dasein's being'. Dasein, as it has fallen into 'the one's' being, 'is proximally and for the most part lost in that with which it concerns itself' (SZ 424/477). It is 'busy'. This busyness is 'explicitly' governed by the use of the clock, which Dasein employs so as to reckon with time efficaciously.

[35] 'Why could time-structures as elemental as those of significance and datability remain hidden from the traditional time concept? Why did it overlook them and why did it have to overlook them?' (BPP 263); 'We should . . . be able to explain . . . *why* the vulgar understanding of time either overlooks or does not suitably understand time's essential structural moments' (BPP 268, translation modified).

[36] 'The covering up of the specific structural moments of world-time, the covering up of their origination in temporality, and the covering up of temporality itself – all have their ground in that mode of being of the Dasein which we call *falling*' (BPP 271).

This use, which is 'public', regulated by 'the one', *distances* Dasein from time's originary modes, *including authentic temporality*, the openness to death-as-what-comes-to-Dasein. Heidegger writes that in its busyness Dasein 'flee[s] in the face of death' and 'look[s] away from the end of being-in-the-world' (SZ 424/477).

By thinking of death, Dasein comes to think of both its finitude and its mineness, for death is not only the end, but also an occurrence 'specific' to 'my' Dasein. It is not the thinking of death in general that will make Dasein seize its possibilities and exist authentically. Only the thinking of its own death can accomplish this. As Heidegger writes, '"the one" never dies because it *cannot* die; for death is in each case mine' (SZ 425/477). Consequently, by looking away from death, two things happen to Dasein: (a) it 'forgets its own essential finitude' (BPP 273) and (b) it forgets its 'mineness'. *'The one' desires both of these.*

What motivates this desire is that Dasein's thinking of its finitude and mineness *disrupts* 'the one's' functioning. For 'the one' to be maintained, Dasein *must* behave as if it belongs to the 'infinite' or 'eternal' being of the *public* or 'universal' 'one'. 'The one' is eternally 'busy' and Dasein's thinking of its finitude forces it to *stop* being busy and reflect on its existence. Moreover, 'the one' is public or 'universal' and Dasein's thinking of its *mineness* forces it to oppose itself to 'the one'. In order, therefore, to maintain itself, 'the one' desires Dasein's 'looking away' from death and thinking of itself in terms of infinity and universality.

'The one' settles for the vulgar instead of the originary conception of time because *its survival depends upon Dasein's fleeing in the face of death*.[37] Science and philosophy appropriate the vulgar conception of time because, being extensions of 'the one', they react against Dasein's finitude and 'individuality'. They suppress these in order to shield 'the one's' infinity and universality.

In its everydayness, in which it 'falls' into 'the one's' being, Dasein is concerned with its being and the being of the other entities in a way that is determined by the 'looking-away' from its finitude and mineness (SZ 424/477). This entails 'looking-away' from *originary time*, Dasein's temporality, which includes, in its authentic mode, the openness to death-as-what-comes-to-Dasein (SZ 424/477). The result of this 'looking-away' from temporality is the strengthening of time's 'infinity' and 'universality' in 'public life', but also in

[37] 'Everydayness . . . as that particular temporality which flees in the face of futuricity, can only be understood when confronted with the *authentic* time of the futural being of the past [i.e. death]' (CT 19, my emphasis).

philosophy and science. This annihilates the openness to death in the 'public sphere', philosophy, and science and thereby secures 'the one's' survival.

In an everydayness in which the openness to death is incessantly suppressed, 'the one' develops various elements prohibiting its uncovering. It promotes the idea that there will *always* be time and that what matters is not what happens to 'my' Dasein but rather what happens in the 'eternal' 'public' space (SZ 425/477). Actions in the public sphere never cease, the one succeeds the other, even if 'my' Dasein dies. *My* death does not matter, as it takes place outside the public domain. Time in everydayness never ends, is uninterrupted, and belongs to 'everyone', not to individual existence (SZ 425/477).

Heidegger's contention is that the 'abstract' now, which reigns in everydayness and determines 'the one's' behaviour, has its 'origin' in temporality. This holds because the now's 'abstraction' is *caused* by the looking-away *from death*, by 'the one's' fleeing *from the openness to death*. That is, infinity appears in 'the one's' life precisely because *the openness to death* is blocked (SZ 425/477–478).

Heidegger has claimed that the vulgar conception of time reigns in 'the world' because therein reigns 'the one', which controls Dasein since it has been 'thrown' into it. But why does '*the one*' espouse the vulgar conception of time instead of the originary one? This happens because 'the one's' survival, its very being, depends upon its 'looking away' from death. The now's 'abstraction' and the covering up of authentic temporality is the *result* of this 'looking-away' from death. It has thus been shown that the vulgar conception of time is *based* on the originary conception of time and, therefore, that the latter's 'originary' status is *justified* (SZ 426/478; BPP 268–269).

## 1.7 Conclusion

### *1.7.1 The 'Vulgar' Understanding of Time*

Heidegger segregates time's 'originary' understanding from its 'vulgar' understanding. The latter conceives time in such a way that its connection with Dasein's comportment in 'the world' is expelled from its 'essential determinacy'. In contrast to time-reckoning, world-time, and temporality, now-time is nothing but a succession of *instantaneous*, *purified*, *numerical* nows. 'The one', which controls Dasein's everydayness, but also traditional philosophy and science, adopted and cultivated the vulgar understanding of time and came to regard now-time as what time 'originarily' is. Heidegger's thesis is that this mode of time is the least 'originary' of all: it 'derives' from time-reckoning, world-time, and, ultimately, temporality.

There are two crucial steps in Heidegger's argument. First, he claims that the vulgar conception of time reads the nature of time off the clock's *use*. As soon as this is accepted, the grounding of now-time is put in the sphere of *Dasein*'s being.[38] Connected to this is Heidegger's insistence that the vulgar conception relates to 'how what we call time becomes *accessible* [to Dasein]' (BPP 256). Second, he explains the 'decision' to read the nature of time off the use of the clock as the tendency to 'look away' from death or non-being.

### 1.7.2 Time and Dasein

At the end of *Basic Problems*, Heidegger declares that 'all ontological propositions are Temporal[39] propositions' (BPP 324). By this he only means that the understanding of being (ontology), because (a) it belongs to Dasein's 'basic constitution' and (b) this constitution is grounded in temporality (Dasein's 'originary constitution'), is itself grounded in temporality. To say that the understanding of being is grounded in temporality is to say that it is 'historical' and 'finite', that it relates to a specific 'world', specific actions, and specific projections, all belonging to a specific, 'epochal' Dasein. In general, for Heidegger, 'all time belongs essentially to the Dasein' (BPP 262; see also CT 13–14: 'Dasein . . . *is time itself*, not *in* time'; CT 21: 'Time is Dasein'), which is 'temporal', namely finite and historical. This contrasts with traditional ontology, which 'go[es] so far as to say that . . . the essentialities, the determination of beings in their being . . . is extratemporal, supratemporal, timeless' (BPP 324). In short, for Heidegger, *because Dasein is temporal (historical)*, the understanding of being is temporal (historical) as well.

Heidegger professes also that the enquiry into the meaning of being cannot begin with *being*, but only with *beings* in the world. This holds because Dasein, to whose basic constitution the understanding of being belongs, comports itself 'at first and for the most part' towards beings in the world (BPP 325; CP 2).[40] As Heidegger puts it, 'for what we experience first and foremost is beings . . . we recognize being only later or maybe even not at all' (BPP 324). He also writes that 'Dasein comports itself directly only to beings' (BPP 322).

[38] Heidegger writes that his notion of the vulgar conception of time being derived from the clock's use 'has pointed our inquiry in the direction of Dasein, if by Dasein we mean that entity in its Being which we know as human life' (CT 6).

[39] Heidegger distinguishes between Temporality (*Temporalität*) and temporality (*Zeitlichkeit*), but this distinction does not affect our discussion. As he puts it, Temporality 'means temporality insofar as temporality itself is made into a theme as the condition of the possibility of the understanding of being and of ontology as such' (BPP 228).

[40] This is entailed by the fact that Dasein is fundamentally being-in-the-world (CT 7).

This does not mean that Dasein's comportment towards beings can occur without its already understanding being.[41] The point, rather, is that in everydayness (which is the starting point of the phenomenological enquiry) Dasein's understanding of being is implicit, hidden, unconscious. Heidegger writes that in its comportment towards beings 'Dasein knows nothing about its having already understood being' and that 'being has the character of the prius which the human being, who is familiar first and foremost merely with beings, has forgotten' (BPP 326).

For Heidegger, our 'recollection' of our understanding of *being* necessarily happens *through* our understanding of *beings*, which comes 'first'.[42] The analysis of our understanding of beings ('the existential analytic of Dasein') leads to *Dasein*'s originary constitution, temporality. It is through this that ontology is disclosed.[43] This is why 'the center of development of ontological enquiry in general lies in the exposition of *the Dasein*'s temporality' (BPP 327, my emphasis). Heidegger stresses that 'no understanding of being is possible that would not root in a comportment toward beings' (BPP 327). Dasein's comportment towards beings has the 'originary constitution' of temporality. But since that comportment contains, in a hidden, implicit manner, the understanding of being, temporality is the ground of all ontology.

## 2 Heidegger's Reading and Critique of Hegel

### 2.1 Introduction

Heidegger discusses Hegel's conception of time in some early texts, notably (a) *Logic: The Question of Truth* (hereafter *Logic*), (b) *Being and Time*, and (c) *Hegel's Phenomenology of Spirit* (hereafter *Hegel's Phenomenology*). *Logic* is the manuscript of a lecture course delivered in 1925–6 and Hegel's conception of time is considered therein in §§20–21. Heidegger's reflections on Hegel's understanding of time in *Being and Time* transpire in §82, the book's penultimate section. Finally, Heidegger invokes time sparingly in *Hegel's Phenomenology*, a lecture course delivered in 1930–1, but in §13b he discusses Hegel's notion of time extensively.

In this section I intend, based on these texts, to draw the picture of early Heidegger's reading and critique of Hegel apropos the problematic of time. In

41 'Since it exists, the Dasein understands being and comports itself toward beings' (BPP 319); 'All comportment toward beings already understands being' (BPP 325).

42 Heidegger speaks of one's 'negotiating the passage from the ontical consideration of beings to the ontological thematization of being' (BPP 227).

43 'Due to the ontical-ontological priority of the Dasein, its being that being which, among all beings, has understanding-of-being, . . . only by ontological analysis of the Dasein can we elucidate the conditions of possibility of a truly conceptualized understanding-of-being, that is to say, ontology, as science of being' (Hofstadter 1982: xi).

particular, I argue that *Heidegger*'s account consists of two steps: (a) The first step endeavours to establish, via a discussion of how Hegel conceives the connection between *space* and time (call this 'the dialectic of space'), that Hegel's treatment of *time* in his philosophy of nature (time's proper locus in the Hegelian system, according to Heidegger) reveals it as *now-time*.[44] This outcome manifests the difference between Hegel's conception of time and Heidegger's and allows Heidegger to *then* employ the transcendental-phenomenological argument expounded in Section 1 in order to certify the superiority of his theory of time to Hegel's. This first step occurs in *Logic* (§§20–21) and §82a of *Being and Time*.

(b) The second step asks about Hegel's view of the relation between time (independently of whether it is now-time or temporality) and *the understanding of being* (*ontology*), an issue remaining unexamined in the first step, and answers that, for Hegel, contra Heidegger, it is not time that is the ground of ontology but rather an element Hegel calls 'the concept'. For Hegel, Heidegger thinks, 'the concept' is the whole of being ('the absolute') and time determines *only a part* or *dimension* of this whole. As time is *only a part* of 'the concept', it follows that *timelessness* (time's 'disappearance') characterizes some other part or dimension of it. So while, for Heidegger, time (temporality) is the sole ground of the understanding of being, for Hegel, not only time but also timelessness grounds such an understanding. This second step in Heidegger's discussion of Hegel's theory of time, which clarifies that Heidegger's dispute with Hegel is *not only* about the nature of time *but also* about the nature of the ground of ontology, materializes in §82b of *Being and Time* and §13b of *Hegel's Phenomenology*.

## 2.2 The Dialectic of Space (I): The Being of Space Is Time

Heidegger's understanding of Hegel's conception of time is driven by his belief that its systematic locus is Hegel's philosophy of nature, the second part of his *Encyclopedia of the Philosophical Sciences in Outline* (hereafter *Encyclopedia*) (Logik 251/208). Hegel refers to time elsewhere too, yet these references are not systematic and thus do not weigh the same as its treatment in philosophy of nature.

In the Western tradition of philosophy of nature, from Aristotle to Kant, time is taken to be connected with space (Logik 251/209) and these two are considered the pillars of nature. *Conjunction*, according to Heidegger, is their traditional connection: there is space 'and also' time (Logik 251–252/209). Heidegger notices that Hegel differs. He deems their connection one of

[44] Heidegger thus 'proves' that Aristotle's 'interpretation' of time 'breaks through' in Hegel (BPP 231).

*becoming* (rather than one of conjunction): space 'becomes' time (Logik 252/209; cf. Enz II §257 Zusatz/34). The *clarification* of this 'becoming', resulting in time's characterization as *now-time*, can be tagged 'the dialectic of space'.

Heidegger maintains that, in Hegel's view, philosophy aims at 'sublating' (*hebt auf*) all difference and hence the difference between space and time (Logik 252/209). Being the sphere of 'absolute thought' (*absolutes Denken*), philosophy accentuates the 'identity' in a relation. This accentuation shows itself in the use of the 'method' of 'dialectic', which Heidegger calls a 'sophistry'. Dialectic is the 'tool' 'absolute thought' employs to undermine the given difference between space and time and showcase their 'identity' (Logik 252/209).

Given this pursuit of 'identity', Heidegger avers, Hegel's statement 'space becomes time' is meant to express the 'sublation' of the difference between space and time and hence to assert their 'identity'. So 'space becomes time' should be understood as meaning that space 'is' time (Logik 252/209). The becoming of time from space, then, does *not* mean that space is independent of or prior to time and gives rise to time. Yet, Heidegger adds, it also does *not* mean that there is no space but only time (Logik 252–253/210). Nor does it mean that 'time' can substitute 'space' in sentences *salva veritate*. Can we speak of time instead of space and still say what we mean to say? Obviously, we cannot. We cannot ask 'how much time does this land occupy?' instead of 'how much space does this land occupy?' 'Space becomes time' means rather that 'space has the being of time' (Logik 253/210). But what does *this* mean?

'Space has the being of time' means that 'the being of space is determined through (*durch*) time, indeed [that it] is determinable *only* from (*aus*) time' (Logik 253/210, translation modified). Space, then, can be what it is only if it exists 'through' or 'from' time. Time is not 'the same' as space, but rather *that which makes* space *possible*. It is space's condition of possibility. This is what the 'is' in 'space is time', their 'identity', means. It means that '*deep down*' space is time, *just because* without time there can be no space.

That which makes something else possible is called by Hegel its 'truth', but also its 'being' (Logik 253/210). That is to say, something's *being* lies in its *truth* (its condition of possibility). So space's being is time because its truth, that which makes it possible, is time. But *how* does time make space possible?[45]

## 2.3 The Dialectic of Space (II): The Nature of the Point

Heidegger begins to show how, for Hegel, time makes space possible by focusing on Hegel's definition of space as 'the unmediated equal validity[46] of

[45] Heidegger writes that, for Hegel, time is the 'explanation' of space (Logik 255/212).
[46] See Kaufmann et al. (2021).

nature's self-externality' (*die vermittlungslose Gleichgültigkeit des Außersichseins der Natur*) (Logik 253/210, translation modified. Heidegger modifies Hegel's text slightly; see Enz II §254/28). Heidegger 'clarifies' this definition as meaning that space is the abstract manyness (*Vielheit*) of the points being differentiable (*unterscheidbaren*) in it (*SZ* 429/481; Logik 253/210). How does the 'manyness of points' derive from the definition of space? Heidegger implies that such 'manyness' derives from nature's *Außersichsein*. Indeed, if something is outside itself, *not only* the given 'something' must be posited *but also* that which is outside it (Kaufmann et al. (2021: 119)).

The many points comprising space are said to be 'equally valid' (*gleichgültig*). This has a twofold significance. On the one hand, it means that no point is privileged: all points are simply aside-one-another (*Nebeneinander*). On the other hand, it means that they are 'indifferent' (*indifferent*) to one another, that they are the same, namely *space* (SZ 429/481; Logik 253/210). This second aspect of their 'equal validity' Heidegger calls 'abstract'. The points' manyness is 'abstract' when it collapses into sameness. This collapse is unavoidable, for each point *is* space. Heidegger articulates this by writing that 'space is not interrupted by these [points] because the points themselves are already space' (Logik 253/210; see also SZ 429/481).

The points' 'equal validity' in space creates a *paradox*. On the one hand, the points, being *many*, are *different* from one another. It is thus that they are able to determine or 'differentiate' space (Logik 253/210). On the other hand, the points, each being *space*, are the same. In this way, space proves to be 'without differences' (*unterschiedslos*) (SZ 429/481; Logik 253/210). So space is both differentiated and undifferentiated, both determinate and indeterminate. Heidegger encapsulates this paradox in the statement that 'the differences themselves are of the same character as that which they differentiate' (SZ 429/481; Logik 253/210–211).

When a point differentiates space and thereby 'interrupts' its unity or oneness, the point *negates* space (Logik 253/211). Yet this happens in such a way that space *remains* (*SZ* 429/481; Logik 253/211). Heidegger writes that even though it undeniably negates space, the point 'does not get out of space' 'as if it were something other than space' (SZ 429/481, translation modified; Logik 253/211). If this holds, though, space's negation must *in turn* be negated. This *negation of negation*, this 'for itself' of negativity, as Hegel calls it, does *not* derive from something other than the point, for there is nothing else here than the point: it is the point itself that both negates space and negates this negation. But since the point, as space, is negated, the space re-emerging when the negation of space is negated is *another* point. In this way, there arises the manyness of points constituting space. This draws the common picture of space being constituted by points which are 'merely limitations of space' (Logik 253/211). That is to say, a point's positing in space does *not* end space; it is rather *perpetually* followed by *another* point.

*Any* point, then, *is* (a) negation of space *and* (b) negation of this negation. This structure of the point Hegel calls 'pointness' (*Punktualität*) (*Enz* II §254, Zusatz/29, my translation; *SZ* 429/481; Logik 254, 260). Pointness, not a specific point, is 'the truth' of space. In order for space to be 'the unmediated equal validity of nature's self-externality', the aside-one-another (*Nebeneinander*) or 'manyness' of points, it *has to* be 'pointness'. Pointness, however, has, for Hegel, the structure of *time* (Enz II §257/33–34; Logik 254/211). So *time* is the condition of the possibility of space and, therefore, *time* is 'the truth' of space. Yet *why* does pointness have the structure of *time*? In what sense of 'time' is pointness temporal?

## 2.4 The Dialectic of Space (III): From the *Nebeneinander* to the *Nacheinander*

The connection between pointness ('the negativity of the point') and time is achieved via an 'interpretation' (Logik 254/211) of this excerpt from Hegel's *Philosophy of Nature*:

> Negativity, which relates as point to space . . . is, though, in the sphere of self-externality also *for itself* (*für sich*), yet by positing (*setzend*) its determinations therein (namely in this being-for-itself (*Fürsichsein*)) equally (*zugleich*) as in the sphere of self-externality, thereby appearing (*erscheinend*) as equally valid (*gleichgültig*) against (*gegen*) the quiet (*ruhige*) aside-one-another (*Nebeneinander*). As thus posited for itself, it[47] is *time*. (Enz II §257/33–34, my translation)

What this obscure excerpt imparts is that the point, in order to be as point, must negate not only space but also this negation. This second act, the negation of negation, is the 'for-itself' of the point's negativity. This structure is distinct from the aside-one-another immediately defining space and is *time*'s defining structure. Let us see in detail how Heidegger 'interprets' the excerpt.

The points and their transformations (lines and planes) determine space by limiting it (Logik 254/211). Yet these determinations/limitations *are* space. Heidegger 'interprets' this as saying that space's limitations 'simply subsist' 'in space' (Logik 254/211). As limitations that are *all* in space, space's determinations are *distinct* from one *another*, *negating* thus one *another* (Logik 254/211). This is the 'aside-one-another' defining space in its immediacy. It

[47] In *Logic*, immediately after the 'it', Heidegger adds 'namely this negativity, the point' (Logik 254/211).

exemplifies negation: the points negate one another but they all remain in space as 'equally valid'. This structure is 'quiet' or 'immobile' (Logik 254/211): the points *stand* aside one another in space and thus they limit space and create determinate spaces. The points (limits) do not come to be and pass away.

The points being aside-one-another, though, have a relation to *space*. Their 'aside-one-another-ness' exemplifies not only the negation occurring among them but also *space*'s negation, for space is 'without differences'. Nevertheless, space's limitations *are* themselves space, so its negation has to be negated. Only thus can the points both determine space *and remain in space*. The point, then, proves to have 'in truth' the structure of the negation of negation. This structure 'sublates' the aside-one-another-ness of the points in space (Logik 255/212). This means that the point's 'immobility' is (momentarily) destroyed: for the points to be aside-one-another, each point must *first* 'get out' of space (negation of space) and *then* re-enter it (negation of the negation of space). The point thus becomes *mobile*.

Heidegger writes that the point 'as what is posited is not-yet-that-point and no-longer-this-point' (Logik 255/212). This means that in order for there to be manyness of points in space, their aside-one-another (*Nebeneinander*), the points must be after-one-another (*Nacheinander*). The point being posited is always already a point that is no longer and a point that is not yet. This is so because, without there being a *succession* of points, there could be no simple subsistence of points, points being aside-one-another in space. When a point is posited, it negates space, but because it itself is space, it negates itself and so 'gets out' of space. Yet, precisely because it *is* space, it negates the negation of space and hence of itself and thus 're-enters' space, becoming a new point. This 'process' or 'movement' is a necessary condition of the possibility of the aside-one-another of points in space. While space is immediately the 'paralyzed' subsistence of many points aside-one-another, *time* is the succession of points required for such a subsistence to take place. This is how Heidegger puts it:

> The negation of the simple subsistence of the point, the being-of-sublation (*das Aufgehobensein*) of pointness as equally valid is a not-remaining-lying (*Nicht-liegen-bleiben*) in the 'paralyzed' quietness (*Ruhe*) of space and the active determining (*fortziehende Bestimmen*) of each point – now here, now here, now here, and so on. This constant negating of the negation is time. (Logik 255/212, my translation)

The 'being-of-sublation' of pointness is the 'not-remaining-lying' in the 'simple subsistence of the point'. Crucially, this is 'time' *because* it has the structure of *succession* or 'active' determining. Time, then, is signified as the *succession* of points. It means to posit a here (a point), to negate it, to negate this negation, *and do the same 'constantly'*. What makes this a succession is *precisely* that each here is a *now*. If it were not a now, all the heres would be *self-sufficiently* aside-one-another. The now prevents this self-sufficiency of the aside-one-another-ness and forces the heres to *follow* one another *in order to be aside-one-another*.

Significantly, Heidegger contrasts this 'dialectical' transition from space to time, a transition occurring by means of *thought* (*Denken*), with the 'experience' (*Erfahrung*) or 'representation' (*Vorstellung*) of space (Logik 254/212). He writes that the representation of space 'immediately' (*unmittelbar*) confirms space as *solely* the realm of simple negation, limitation, and determination, to wit, as *solely* the realm of aside-one-another (Logik 254/212). In Hegel's view, Heidegger argues, such a confirmation does not make the points' aside-one-another-ness the 'being' of space (Logik 254/212), as such a 'being' can only be grasped in thought (Logik 255/212). Thought, as seen, does *not* confirm space as simple negation, as the realm of equally valid points that have *self-sufficiently* an immediate subsistence as aside-one-another. Precisely because thought is the power of negation, it negates space's immediate determinations and thereby discloses it as the negation of negation. Being represented, the point is negation (limitation); being thought, it is pointness, the negation of negation. Through thought, negation (the 'equally valid' points in space) is 'sublated' (*Logik* 255/212). Thus, exactly because the point not only determines space but also is determined through thought, when it is posited, it is itself negated. As seen, the point's negation posits *another point*, a new self-externality (Logik 255/212), *and so* space is the manyness of points.

Space's 'truth' or 'being', then, amounts to a *process* (*Prozeß*) (*Logik* 261/217), in which the point, the 'here', functions as the negation of space, but then it is itself negated (the negation of negation). Each 'here' is realized in a *sequence* or as an after-one-another (*Nacheinander*). Consequently, the sequence or succession *belongs* to the 'here' or the aside-one-another (*Nebeneinander*). For such a sequence to *be*, the 'heres' must be determined *temporally*, as 'nows': *now* the 'here' is posited as space, *now* it functions as space's negation, *now* this negation is negated. For the 'here' to exist qua 'here', then, it has to be 'now-here' (Logik 255–256/212).

Time is presented as the succession (rather than the simple subsistence), the after-one-another (rather than the aside-one-another), of points. A succession of points is based on each point (a here) being a now, for if it were not a now, there would be only an unconditioned simple subsistence of points (which, given 'pointness', is an impossibility). Heidegger stresses that *succession* is, for Hegel, a necessary condition of the possibility of a *simple subsistence* of points. So time, as a succession of nows, the *Nacheinander*, is a necessary condition of the possibility of space, the *Nebeneinander*.

## 2.5 Time and Logos

### *2.5.1 Hegel, Heidegger and 'The Problematic of Temporality'*

The dialectic of space has established that, for Hegel, (a) the 'truth' of space is time and (b) time is the succession of nows. This conception of time, 'now-time',[48] is, as seen, what Heidegger calls 'the vulgar conception of time'. He considers the view that (a) this shows 'unambiguously' that, for Hegel, time is the ground of (the understanding of) *being* and that (b) as soon as now-time has emerged, Hegel could 'derive' it from 'temporality'. If this held, Hegel's position would come dangerously close to Heidegger's. As Heidegger puts it, 'Hegel determines the being of space as time. And so one might ask: [1] Is being here not quite unambiguously determined from time (*aus der Zeit*)? [2] Is it not absolutely clear, then, that Hegel operates in the problematic of temporality?' (Logik 256/213, translation modified). Heidegger wants to respond negatively to both these questions and thus prove that Hegel 'is light-years away from' his own position (Logik 256/213).

### *2.5.2 Time as 'Intuited Becoming'*

Let me begin with his negative response to the *second question*. To justify this response, he delves into Hegel's *explanation of now-time*. Space, for Hegel, is grounded in now-time, but wherein is *now-time* grounded? Heidegger aspires to show that Hegel's answer does not involve 'temporality' and hence differs from his own. As he expresses it, 'Hegel ... does not understand its [i.e. time's] temporal function' (Logik 256/213) and 'as regards temporality, there is nothing to expect and learn from Hegel' (Logik 257/214, translation modified).

Heidegger observes that Hegel grounds now-time in *intuited becoming* (*angeschautes Werden*) (SZ 431/482; Logik 258/214; Enz II §258/34). Intuited becoming has two components: (a) becoming and (b) intuition and, importantly, Heidegger attends to *both* of them. Let me tackle these in turn.

### *2.5.3 Becoming*

Becoming is a *logical* category, a category of 'pure thought', leading Heidegger to Hegelian *logic*, the domain of (pure) *logos*.[49] There Hegel defines

---

[48] Heidegger provides 'further explicit evidence' that Hegel understands time as now-time on Logik 257–258/214–215. This 'evidence' amounts to citations from Enz II §§258–259/34–40. He accentuates the following in Hegel's conception of time: the priority of the now, the now's constant disappearance, becoming as 'the concept' of time, and the emphasis on passing-away (rather than on coming-to-be).

[49] De Boer writes that, according to Heidegger, Hegel's conception of time is 'independent' of 'the concept' and that this is a mistaken interpretation. In De Boer's view, 'Hegel's concept of time is not independent, but is grounded in the structure of the concept as that is unfolded in the *Logic*'

'becoming' as the 'transition' from being to nothing and vice versa (WL I 83/SL 60). Precisely because becoming is *such* a transition, Heidegger stresses that it 'is both coming-to-be and passing-away' (SZ 431/482). The fluctuation from being to nothing and vice versa, namely becoming, is simply another name for 'the negation of negation', which, as seen, is involved in now-time. Being is posited, but it is immediately negated, only for this negation to be negated, resulting in a new positing of being.

Becoming is *not* now-time. It is only the *logos* involved in now-time. A now cannot succeed another now unless there is transition from being to nothing and vice versa. So 'transition' is *not* a *temporal* element. It is the logical element enabling time. Without 'becoming', there would be stillness, not a succession of nows.

Logos or 'pure thought', therefore, 'underlies' now-time. But if now-time (a) is *not* identified with becoming but (b) involves it, what is it that is *added* to becoming for now-time to arise? Logos only gives the formula of transition grounding succession in general. For this reason, succession is not a structure immediately generating *specifically* now-time. For a *now* to be posited, something else must underlie now-time besides logos (becoming).

### *2.5.4 Intuition*

The now is provided by intuited becoming's second component: *intuition.* When something is intuited, it is immediately experienced as being *now.*[50] Moreover, intuition presents *only* the now as *being.* For Hegel, then, in the structure of time only the now is. This is a consequence of his declaration that time is not only becoming (logos, pure thought) but also intuition (Enz II §259 Zusatz/39; Logik 258/214–215). *As intuition*, time is 'the transition, *which is not thought* but which is *simply provided* in the succession of nows' (SZ 431/483, my translation and emphasis). This means that, *as intuition*, time has its being in the succession of *nows* (Logik 260/216). There cannot be time without intuition, for the *nows* cannot be without intuition.

Heidegger then acknowledges that, for Hegel, 'the concrete' cannot emerge from *sheer* logos; it requires also the involvement of an element that is *not* logos, namely 'intuition'. Nevertheless, in Heidegger's view, this does not undermine the 'impulse' (*Trieb*) of Hegelian philosophy towards 'identity'.[51]

---

(De Boer 2000: 261). De Boer is wrong on this, as, for Heidegger, Hegel's notion of time is *indeed* grounded (partially) in logic.

50 'The term "intuition" speaks for this interpretation because it refers to an immediate contact with something present now' (Schmidt 1988: 47–48); '"intuited" means experience in its individuality, and this individuality is the now' (Logik 258/214).

51 See Trisokkas (2022b: 358) and WL II.555/SL 739.

Intuition discloses being qua nature only if it is 'formed' by 'pure thought'. In the ontology of nature (i.e. the understanding of being as nature), intuition, albeit present, is subordinated to logos.

Intuition is the 'source' of 'immediacy', 'individuality', and 'content' in *formed* nature. It is that which, when added to logos or 'the *pure* concept', makes specific natural phenomena *perceivable* (rather than understandable). *Time* is a natural, rather than a *simply* logical phenomenon, because it requires not only 'pure thought' but also intuition. It is true, Heidegger points out, that Hegel identifies 'the *concept* of time' with 'becoming' (Logik 258/215). But this shows only that Hegel's own 'real' concept of time as 'intuited becoming', namely *time itself*, time as a structure of the understanding of being qua *nature*, should *not* be identified with what is 'pure' or 'logical' in time. 'Intuited becoming' is only the result of the 'realization' or 'schematization' of the pure concept of becoming through its connection with intuition.

Crucially, Heidegger claims that the intuition involved in the determination of *time* is, for Hegel, a *pure* intuition (SZ 431/483). By this he means simply that, for Hegel, the now is not the world-time now or the now engendered by enpresenting (recall the discussion in Section 1). It is, rather, the 'naked' now of now-time. Heidegger suggests that this is so because, in Hegel, the intuition involved in the specification of the now is 'abstract' rather than practical. Hegel's 'now' is not the 'now' of Heidegger's temporality: the latter, as seen, has a practical content and is 'ready-to-hand' (*zuhanden*), the former is purified from such a content and is 'present-at-hand' (*vorhanden*) (SZ 431/483; Logik, 258, 260/215–216). Hegel's notion of time is the highest of abstractions because it combines the 'formal-empty schema' of logical becoming with *pure* intuition (Logik 261/217).[52]

It is significant to emphasize that this 'pure intuition', whatever it is, is *not* a logical element. It is something, in Heidegger's words, 'simply provided' to logos by experience or empirical representation (including 'empirical physics'; see Enz II §246 Remark/6). In Kant, time is the pure form of empirical intuition that connects with pure thought (in particular, 'the pure understanding') for experience to occur. Heidegger seems to say that Hegel thinks differently: time is the *result* of the connection between pure thought and pure intuition. It might also be significant to stress that the involvement of intuition in the structure of time in particular and in philosophy of nature in general makes it clear that, for Heidegger, the domain of Hegel's philosophy of nature is a domain of thought, just like logic is. To the question 'who intuits in Hegel's philosophy of nature?' Heidegger would say 'thought'.

[52] Heidegger accuses idealism in general of proceeding by means of a 'free-floating construction' (SZ 27–28/49–50).

All in all, Heidegger has argued that, for Hegel, now-time 'derives' from a combination of logos and 'pure' intuition rather than from 'temporality'. From this, Heidegger deduces that 'Hegel moves wholly in the direction of the vulgar understanding of time' (SZ 431/483) and hence that Hegel's theory of time does not 'operate in the problematic of temporality'. In this way, Heidegger has responded to the *second* question he raised.

### 2.5.5 The Timelessness of Pure Logos

This conclusion has a ramification pertaining to Heidegger's *first* question, namely whether, for Hegel, *being* is determined 'from time'. It has been shown that, for Hegel, there cannot be now-time without 'becoming', which is a *logical* category. Heidegger's view of 'logos's' relation to 'being' in Hegel is ambiguous. Sometimes he suggests that, for Hegel, 'being' is reduced to pure logos, while other times he recognizes that, for Hegel, 'being' consists of pure logos, nature, and spirit. Fortunately, we do not need to resolve this difficult issue. It suffices that Heidegger takes Hegel to say that pure logos is (at least) one dimension of being. Since, in Hegel's system, pure logos does not *reduce* to nature, pure logos is *not* determined by time (for time 'belongs' to nature). *It follows* that pure logos is determined by timelessness. But if logos is (a) determined by timelessness and (b) is a dimension of being, then it cannot be said that, for Hegel, being is 'determined from time'. This answers Heidegger's *first* question in the negative.

### 2.5.6 Eternity and the Timelessness of the Logical Categories

In this section we have seen how Heidegger argues for the claim that *Hegel*'s conception of time is 'vulgar'. This conception of time, *now-time*, which has emerged from Hegel's 'dialectic of space', is grounded, not in temporality, but in logos and 'pure' intuition. Since logos, a dimension of being, is distinct from nature and time belongs solely to nature, ontology is not determined solely 'from time'. It is *precisely* for this reason that Heidegger writes that 'even when he characterizes time as becoming, Hegel understands this becoming in an "abstract" sense, which goes well beyond the representation of the "stream" of time' (SZ 432/483).

'Becoming' 'goes well beyond' the succession of nows (the 'stream' of time) because, as a logical structure, it, *by itself,* exemplifies timelessness rather than now-time (recall that 'becoming' is only *one* of the constituents of time, the other being intuition). This timelessness, exemplified by logical categories (HPG 205/142), pervades nature and forms it, thus giving it determinacy. As an element pervading nature, the timelessness of logos is called by Hegel 'infinity' or 'eternity' (SZ 431/483; Logik 258/214). This infinity is not something that excludes time (how could this be possible given that 'becoming' is involved in time?); it is rather something enabling time. 'Infinity' and 'eternity', therefore, *in this specific sense*, should not be identified with 'the succession of nows' in Hegel's ontology, although this succession is sometimes also called 'infinity' and 'eternity'. They signify something entirely different: the timelessness of the logical categories.

What is most important in all of this is that, in Heidegger's reading, (pure) logos is, for Hegel, timeless, 'infinite', or 'eternal'. Given that pure logos is a dimension of being, the understanding of being is not grounded solely in time, is not solely historical, but requires also the involvement of timelessness, seeing things *sub specie aeternitatis*.[53]

## 2.6 Time and Absolute Being

### 2.6.1 The Disagreement About the Nature of the Understanding of Being

I will complete this section by taking a closer look at Heidegger's account of Hegel's idea of the relation between 'absolute being' or 'the concept' and time. In *Logic*, Heidegger comments that all Hegel's dialectic of space shows is that time is the ground of *the being of space*, not the ground of *the whole being*, what he calls, following Hegel, 'absolute being' (Logik 256/213). Crucially, he recognizes that where Hegel expounds being 'in general' (*Sein überhaupt*), in logic, time is absent (Logik 257/213). Thus, it is not simply that Heidegger's early 'confrontation' with Hegel amounts to a disagreement about the nature of *time*. They disagree also about the nature of the understanding of *being*, whether being is understood solely 'from time' or *timelessness* is also involved in ontological understanding.

### 2.6.2 Heidegger on the Relation Between the Concept, Time and Spirit in Hegel

In §82b of *Being and Time*, Heidegger reflects on the relation between time (and nature in general), spirit, and 'the concept'. The concept, which is, in its purity, a *logical* structure (logos, the categories), *forms* both time (nature) and spirit. There is a difference between the two formations, though. While the concept forms nature independently of self-consciousness, it forms spirit in the manner of self-consciousness. Indeed, spirit *is* logos itself striving to become *conscious of itself* in nature (SZ 434/485; cf. HPG 32–33/23). Heidegger observes that, for Hegel, both nature and spirit are in time, *but* spirit is in time because, as Hegel

[53] Markus Gabriel judges Heidegger's reading of Hegel in an exceedingly negative way: as a 'misrepresentation' and a 'failure', as 'mistaken', 'erroneous', and 'misguided' (Gabriel 2021: 344). Others share the same view; see Trivers (1942), Von der Luft (1989), Williams (1989: 141–142), and Houlgate (2006b: 125–132). Yet, in my view, Heidegger has simply followed Hegel's 'dialectic of space' to its logical conclusion, now-time, and drawn the ramifications of *Hegel*'s determination of now-time as 'intuited becoming'. It is difficult to see from Gabriel's discussion what exactly *justifies* his ultra-negative evaluation.

himself puts it (VG 133), it 'falls into' time (i.e. into nature) (SZ 428/480) and that this 'falling' is possible because they share 'the concept' (logos) as a common structure (SZ 434/485). 'The concept' (*logos*), nature (an element formed by *logos* without self-consciousness) and spirit (*logos* conscious of itself in nature) comprise 'the system', which exhibits the understanding of *being*.[54] As the concept *forms* nature (time) and spirit, it covers the *whole* of being. As *pure* concept, it covers being's logical dimension. In this dimension, it is characterized by timelessness. As 'schematized' or 'concrete' or 'real' concept, it covers being's natural and spiritual dimensions. In these dimensions, it manifests itself as time.

We saw that, in Heidegger's reading of Hegel, the latter takes time to be grounded in intuited becoming, which involves logos, since 'becoming' is a logical structure. 'Becoming', as seen, is simply another name for 'the negation of negation', the basic function of 'thought'. Since 'thought' forms both time (nature) and spirit, they share the structure of the negation of negation.

Heidegger maintains that Hegel not only *asserts* that spirit falls into time but also *explains* how such a 'falling' is *possible*. Since time's 'essence' or 'ground' has already been determined as the negation of negation, for such an explanation to be provided one has to determine *spirit*'s 'essence' or 'ground'. Heidegger formulates the guiding question in the following way: 'How is spirit itself to be understood in order that it can be said that it accords with it in its realization to fall into time, determined as negation of negation?' (SZ 433/484, translation modified). This explanation will differentiate Heidegger's account of the understanding of being from Hegel's. While, for Heidegger, this understanding is grounded in time, for Hegel, Heidegger claims, it is grounded in logos or 'the pure concept'. For Heidegger, time is ontology's sole horizon. For Hegel, this horizon is 'the pure concept', not time. Precisely *because*, for Hegel, the understanding of being is grounded in the pure concept, spirit (man) 'falls into time'. If there were no such grounding and hence no such 'falling', spirit would *be* time and so Hegel's position would be 'deep down' identical to Heidegger's.

For Hegel, Heidegger stipulates, 'the essence of spirit is *the concept*' (SZ 433/484). The concept, for Hegel, Heidegger writes, is not what is usually meant with this term: it is not the universal element standing for the genus or species of individual representations and deriving from them inductively. It is rather 'the form of thought thinking itself' (*die Form des sich denkenden Denkens*) (SZ 433/484). The 'thought thinking itself' is defined by

[54] Heidegger writes in *Hegel's Phenomenology* that 'the encyclopedia' – that is, 'the system of philosophy' composed of logic, philosophy of nature, and philosophy of spirit – 'contains the whole of metaphysics' (HPG 9/6). See the discussion in Trisokkas (2021; 2022a).

a particular *logical* 'form', an element's *return* to *itself* through *negation*. For *such* return to occur a *double* negation is required: first, the element's negation is posited as its *other* and, second, this negation is negated. This logical or 'formal' structure, 'the concept', *when it 'appears' as spirit*, is transformed into the 'conception' (*Begreifen*) of the 'I' by the 'I' *via the 'not-I'* (nature). Precisely because such a mediation defines spirit, spirit incorporates negation or 'differentiation'. Because, however, this negation is negated, so that the I can think *itself* in the *other* (nature), the I or spirit has the structure of the negation of negation. In other words, spirit, being an appearance of *the concept*, confronts what is not spirit (nature), yet it negates this negation, thereby affirming that its other (nature) is spirit itself. In this way, Heidegger remarks, 'Hegel can define the essence of spirit formally ... as the negation of negation' (SZ 433/484).

The realization that spirit's 'essence' or 'ground' is double negation discloses the *isomorphism* holding between spirit and time, since, as discovered, time has *the same* 'essence' or 'ground'. Heidegger writes that 'because the restlessness with which spirit develops in bringing itself to its concept is the *negation of negation*, it accords with spirit, as it realizes itself, to fall "into time" [conceived] as the immediate *negation of negation*' (SZ 434/485). Double negation is the 'ground' of both time and spirit, but what matters most here is that it exemplifies *logos*. So it is logos or 'thought', 'the transcendental', that is the 'ground' of spirit *and* time. Thus, for Hegel, Heidegger argues, ontology is not grounded solely in time, but involves eternity or timelessness either as a sole or as a necessary ground. This is the main point of Heidegger's discussion in §82b of *Being and Time*.

A final note: In §82b Heidegger refers to a well-known passage from the *Phenomenology* as providing support to his reading of Hegel. This is the passage:

> *Time* is the *concept* itself which *is there* (*da ist*) and represents itself to consciousness as empty intuition (*als leere Anschauung*); because of this spirit appears necessarily in time and it appears in time (*in der Zeit*) as long as (*so lange*) it does not *conceive* its own pure concept, that is to say, as long as it does not annul (*tilgt*) time. Time is the *external*, intuited, *not conceived* by the self, pure self, the concept which is merely intuited. (PG 584/487, my translation)

Immediately after, Heidegger registers his conclusion: 'Thus *by its very essence* spirit necessarily appears in time' (SZ 434/485).

Heidegger comprehends this passage as follows. Time is *the concept as connected to intuition*, namely the concept as it is 'realized' or 'schematized' in nature. Spirit is the 'realized' concept too, albeit differently than time is (qua spirit the concept is realized through various stages of self-consciousness, qua time/nature it is realized through simple formation of intuition/matter). This is why neither time nor spirit is *pure* logos. Yet, even as schematized, time and spirit remain *the concept* (i.e. they are formed by logos) and this is why spirit *can* 'fall into' time. *As the concept*, spirit is double negation, *as time is too*, and this is what allows it to have a temporal and hence historical character.

Heidegger, while recognizing that Hegel 'puts' spirit 'in time' and hence historicizes the understanding of being, stresses that his own 'historicization' of ontology is different and, crucially, *more 'originary'* than Hegel's. This holds because while, for Heidegger, ontology's ground is temporality (from which historicity necessarily flows), for Hegel, this ground is 'the concept', only one side of which (its 'schematized' or 'realized' side) is determined by time. Its other side is logos or pure thought or 'the transcendental', which is determined by timelessness. As Hegel himself writes, 'time … has no power over the concept' and the concept is 'the power over time' (Enz II §258 Remark/35).

### 2.6.3 Time as Only One 'Way' of Understanding Being

Although the main topic of Heidegger's *Hegel's Phenomenology* is the transition from consciousness to self-consciousness in Hegel's *Phenomenology of Spirit* (hereafter 'the *Phenomenology*'), Heidegger offers brief but, regarding our enquiry, decisive reflections on Hegel's idea of the relation between time and (the understanding of) being.[55] These reflections pertain to the system in general rather than to Hegelian phenomenology in particular.[56] The upshot of Heidegger's deliberations is that Hegel does not regard time as being's sole ground, but only as *one* 'way' of being, and that timelessness or 'infinity' is *another* 'way' of being (maybe the 'primary' or 'originary' 'way'[57]). Hegelian logic expresses this infinity, so it exemplifies a timeless *understanding* of being. This contrasts with Heidegger's fundamental thesis that the ground of *any* understanding of being is time.

To begin with, Heidegger shows early in the text an appreciation of the fact that Hegel's philosophy has the form of a 'system'.[58] The 'system' is 'the way in

[55] In *Hegel's Phenomenology* Heidegger conflates 'being' and 'the understanding of being' (see, e.g., HPG 203/141). It is clear, though, that his concern is with the *understanding* of being and that he takes Hegel to mean (also) this understanding whenever he speaks of 'being'.

[56] This relates to the fact that Hegel's reference to time in the *Phenomenology*'s 'Self-Consciousness' chapter is *not* derived systematically from the 'dialectic's' previous stages. It emerges, as Heidegger remarks, as an *Apposition* (HPG 207/144). This is why Heidegger proceeds to elucidate this reference through a reading of Hegel's 'Jena Manuscripts' (HPG 207–208/144).

[57] Heidegger writes that logic is Hegel's 'essential philosophical work' (HPG 8/6) and that 'the system … has the logic as its only appropriate beginning' (HPG 12/9).

[58] 'The system is not an optional framework or an ordering of absolute knowledge by way of addition. Rather, absolute knowledge is conceived and is exclusively aware of itself only when it unfolds and presents itself in and as system' (HPG 24/17).

which philosophy unfolds itself as absolute knowledge' (HPG14/ 10) and 'absolute knowledge' denotes both our understanding of being and being's fundamental structure.[59] Heidegger acknowledges that the system has three parts, each of which exemplifies a distinct ontological *dimension* (HPG 3–4/ HPS 3). *Logic* displays being's logical dimension (*logos*), *philosophy of nature* exhibits its physical dimension (*nature*), and *philosophy of spirit* presents its spiritual dimension (*spirit*). Crucially, Heidegger stresses that logic *contrasts* with philosophy of nature and philosophy of spirit *taken together*. These two constitute what Hegel calls *Realphilosophie*, 'the philosophy of the concrete' (HPG 3–4/3), whose framework is determined fundamentally by time and space. By contrast, logic's framework is determined fundamentally by *divinity*, 'the ontology of the *ens realissimum*, the highest actuality as such' (HPG 4–5/3). Heidegger insists that 'speculative theology' has shaped Hegelian logic and been united with ontology therein. As he puts it, 'this unity of speculative theology and ontology is the proper concept of Hegelian logic' (HPG 4–5/3).

*Timelessness* defines divinity, so logic, as a field manifesting divinity, is characterized by timelessness or infinity. Therefore, since logic is a part of the system, infinity is established as a fundamental feature of ontology. This, Heidegger notes, reveals the real concern of Hegelian philosophy: it is 'concerned with *overcoming finite knowledge and attaining infinite knowledge*' (HPG 15/11). 'Infinite knowledge' means an understanding of being as timelessness, which entails that this understanding is itself timeless.[60] For Hegel, Heidegger stresses, philosophy strives to overcome finitude and achieves this with logic (HPG 93–94/66). This does not mean that finitude is ostracized from the system (Schmidt 1988: 14–15). Philosophy of nature and philosophy of spirit, as they develop in the framework of time and space, exhibit finite structures of being (cf. Logik 259/215), yet these, precisely because they relate to logos, are finite only as 'moments' of infinity (HPG 54–55/38).

Heidegger writes that being or 'absolute being' (HPG 203/141), in *all* its three dimensions, is, for Hegel, 'the concept' (HPG 17–18/12). The concept, since it has a dimension in which time is absent, is partially timeless or infinite. Heidegger expresses this lucidly:

> [For Hegel,] [t]he concept . . . is the power of time, i.e., *the pure concept annuls time*. In other words, the problem of being is properly conceived only when time is made to disappear. The Hegelian philosophy expresses this

[59] Heidegger writes that in Hegelian logic being 'is grasped *from* the λόγος and *as* λόγος' (HPG 17/ 12; see also HPG 204/141–142).

[60] Heidegger writes that 'that science which knows in an absolute way "knows the absolute"' (HPG 24/17). Similarly, that science which knows timelessness knows it timelessly.

> disappearance of time by conceiving philosophy as *the* science or as absolute knowledge. (HPG 17–18/12)

The concept is 'the power of time' in the sense that the concept dominates time, is more 'originary' than it. Heidegger carefully clarifies that it is the concept's *purity* (logos), not the whole concept, that 'annuls time'. The statement that 'the problem of being is properly conceived only when time is made to disappear' means that, for Hegel, being *cannot* be understood without affirming timelessness. Philosophy is *the* science exactly because along with nature and spirit, materializing in time and space, its subject-matter, *being* ('absolute being'), has a third dimension, logos, in which time disappears.

All this is repeated and reinforced in §13b. Here Heidegger explains that logos or 'the *pure* concept' is the dimension of timelessness in 'absolute being' or 'the concept' and is composed of the pure 'categories' (HPG 205/142). So 'timelessness' is *identical* with 'purity', both designating the structures 'forming' nature and spirit while having an independent 'origin'. 'The pure concept', which 'forms' nature and spirit, provides the latter with *both* multiple categorial formations *and* its defining structure ('form') as '*the* concept', namely *immanent development.* This is a development proceeding by means of one's self-division (and thus the generation of an 'other') and return to the one's unity (HPG 207/143).

Heidegger also explicitly says that, for Hegel, 'life', an expression of *nature,* is *only one* 'way' of being (*eine Weise des Seins*) (HPG 206/143). Heidegger then intimates that, for Hegel, being is said in *many* ways (*λεγεται πολλαχως*). What is, for us, significant is that at this juncture Heidegger refers to *time*, repeating his thesis that, for Hegel, time has its proper locus in philosophy of *nature* (HPG 208/144). If (a) time has its proper locus in nature and (b) nature is *only one* of the 'ways' of 'absolute being', then 'absolute being' *must* have a 'way' in which time 'disappears'.

Heidegger acknowledges that *spirit* or 'the problematic of history' is defined, like nature, *through time* (HPG 208/144). For Hegel, not only nature but also spirit is 'in time'. Yet, Heidegger adds, 'this happens each time in a formal carrying-over of the concept of time, which belongs to the philosophy of nature, to these realms [of spirit and history]' (HPG 208/144, translation modified). Indeed, as Heidegger asserts in *Being and Time*, for Hegel, the relation between time and spirit (history) is 'formal': spirit 'falls into' time.

We must here identify carefully how, *in Heidegger's view*, each of the dimensions of Hegel's 'absolute being' relates to time. (a) *Nature* is determined *from* time, in the sense that the framework in which nature develops and thereby exhibits its determinations has the form of a succession of nows. This 'framework' is not external to nature; it belongs to its very being. (b) *Logos* is beyond time, timeless, or 'infinite'. Its being does not have the character of a succession but rather of a unifying power, gathering disparate elements and unifying them into a single 'thought' or 'being'. (c) Finally, *spirit* is logos that 'falls into' time and, crucially, thereby becomes *conscious* of itself *in nature. This* 'falling' *defines* spirit (but not logos *as such*) and hence belongs to its *essence* or *being*, yet *time*, into which it falls, does *not* belong to it. Time is not a spiritual element. This contrasts with Heidegger's account of the relation between Dasein and time: Dasein, the equivalent, mutatis mutandis, of Hegel's 'spirit', does not 'fall into' time; rather, it *is* time. Time is not 'nature', a succession of nows, but Dasein's temporality.

Heidegger adds a crucial remark: 'The problematic of time is not *primarily* (*primär*) developed in terms of history and even of spirit, for the simple reason that this would run as counter to Hegel's basic intention (*Grundabsicht*) as anything could' (HPG 208/144, my emphasis). 'The problematic of time' would *be* 'primarily developed in terms of history and even of spirit' if spirit did *not* 'fall into' time but rather *were* time (temporality, finitude). That is, *such* development would occur if time, as spirit's temporality, were *the ground* of the understanding of being. Why did Hegel not develop 'the problematic of time' in this way? Heidegger claims that this would run counter to Hegel's 'basic intention'. What is this 'basic intention'? Numerous clues have been given about this. It is the same 'intention' all 'traditional' philosophers share: the 'looking away' from death or non-being, the suppression of finitude's primacy. This is why Hegel *chooses* to make timelessness an ontological dimension.

In §13b of *Hegel's Phenomenology*, Heidegger expressly *contrasts* his thesis about the relation between *being* and *time* with Hegel's. Heidegger's thesis is that 'the essence of being is time' (HPG 209/145). This means that *being is understood through time.* Hegel's thesis is 'the exact opposite': 'being is the essence of time' (HPG 209/145). If it is 'the exact opposite' of Heidegger's thesis, this could only mean that *time is understood through being.*

Heidegger explicates 'being' here as 'infinity' (HPG 209/145), so Hegel's thesis is that time is understood through infinity. What does 'infinity' mean *here*? It *cannot* mean the succession of nows, because, given that, in Heidegger's view, 'time', for Hegel, *is* the succession of nows, Hegel's thesis would be a tautology: the succession of nows is understood through the succession of nows. There is only one other meaning of 'infinity' in Hegel: logos, thought, timelessness, eternity, the purity of the categories holding together (or 'forming') spatio-temporal phenomena. Consequently, Hegel's 'opposite' thesis is that *time is understood through logos*. This entails that time is not the absolute ground of the understanding of being, that, at the most, it is only a part of such a ground and that logos (timelessness) is, at least, another part of it.

All in all, what Heidegger wants to convey in §13b is that, for Hegel, 'time is *one* appearance of the *simple* essence of being *qua* infinity' (HPG 209/145, Heidegger's italics). Time is not the 'origin' of ontological understanding. It is involved in it but only as *one* appearance of being's '*simple* essence'. This simple essence, 'infinity' or 'the concept', has *logos* as its fundamental ingredient. Logos becomes time when *it* is combined with 'pure' intuition and becomes spirit (or 'history' or 'the I') when *it* becomes conscious of *itself* in time. Pure logos (timelessness), nature (time), and spirit (consciousness) are three distinct 'ways' of 'the formal concept of absolute being' (HPG 210/145) that always has logos (thought) present in it.[61]

## 2.7 Conclusion

### 2.7.1 Hegel's Forgetting of Finitude

Section 2 has argued that there are two sides to Heidegger's reading and critique of Hegel. *First*, he reasons that the dialectic of space in Hegel's philosophy of nature discloses time as now-time and that the latter is, according to Hegel, the nature of time (because, Heidegger contends, the proper locus of time is, for Hegel, nature). This view, which Heidegger calls 'vulgar' (Logik 260/216), contrasts with his own understanding of time as 'temporality'. Heidegger's *critique* of Hegel is the same he directs against the vulgar conception of time in general, namely that now-time cannot represent time's 'originary' nature, since it 'derives' from temporality.

*Second*, Heidegger holds that Hegel does not even have time (regardless of whether it is now-time or temporality) as ontology's sole ground. For Hegel, there is an ontological *dimension* in which, as Heidegger puts it, 'time disappears'. Hegel calls this dimension variably 'logos', 'pure thought', and 'the pure concept'. Logos is marked by 'infinity', *but not in the sense of 'succession of nows'*; it rather denotes *a pure (categorial) function of formation*. Hegel's making timelessness an ontological dimension contradicts Heidegger's thesis that temporality is the *sole* ground of *any* understanding of being. Heidegger's *critique* of this Hegelian conception of the relation between time and ontology is that, pace received opinion, Hegel's ontology is not, strictly speaking, historical, but rather a mixture of historical and 'onto-theological' (ahistorical) elements.

[61] Heidegger writes that 'time is one appearance of being in the sphere of that which lacks spirit' (HPG 210/145). This attests for the distinctness of 'the concept's' three dimensions.

Heidegger avows throughout his early corpus that what defines Hegel's work is its attempt to establish 'absolute being' as ontology's sole subject-matter. In this section I have asked what this tells us about Heidegger's view of Hegel's conception of *time*. I have defended the thesis that, for Heidegger, Hegel's position is that time does *not* cover the *whole* domain of 'absolute being', that timelessness also has a presence therein.

What unites the two facets of Heidegger's account of Hegel is the common 'motivation' he sees behind the two Hegelian theses. Both the thesis that the nature of time is now-time and the thesis that the understanding of being involves timelessness are motivated by Hegel's implicit, hidden, 'subterranean', unconscious *desire* to 'forget' finitude, death, the end of being. (Recall that Hegel calls *both* the succession of nows *and* the pure categorial formation 'infinity'.) Hegel, Heidegger avers, shares this desire with common sense, science, and 'traditional' philosophy. In all these domains, finitude becomes only a 'moment' of infinity, the end that is always 'overcome' for being to be maintained.

For Heidegger, finitude cannot be overcome. It is ontology's beginning and end. In *The Concept of Time*, he considers the Hegelian idea that we can understand being through 'eternity' and raises the methodological objection that this conflicts with the necessity of our temporality being a starting point. It is 'fine', he says, to declare that the understanding of being is grounded in 'eternity', but this entails that the starting point is 'eternity' (CT 1). The problem is that such a 'departure' is not 'at our disposal' (CT 1). To understand being through eternity we have to be 'acquainted with eternity and adequately understand it' (CT 1). But we do not have such a relation with eternity to begin with and never can because we are temporal beings determined by finitude and death.

### 2.7.2 Other Issues

I have argued that early Heidegger's critique of Hegel's theory of time is (a) that time is not 'originarily', as Hegel thinks, now-time, but rather 'temporality', and (b) that time is not simply one dimension of the ground of our understanding of being, as Hegel judges, but rather the sole ground of this understanding. Throughout his discussion of Hegel, Heidegger raises a number of other concerns, which I have left out of the limelight. The following are quite significant, but I won't be able to develop them any further.

*First*, Heidegger throughout voices his dissatisfaction with Hegel's 'dialectic', the 'method' of 'thought' (Logik 257/213). 'Dialectic' is problematic, Heidegger argues, because it destroys philosophy's proper starting point, namely 'experience' or 'everydayness'. 'Everydayness' manifests the 'immediacy' of our understanding of being, what Hegel calls 'simple negation'. 'Dialectic' incites the negation of simple negation and thereby obliterates the possibility of a phenomenological reflection on what matters[62] to Dasein 'at first and for the most part'. As a result, Hegel fails to see time's 'temporal' function and thereby 'misinterprets time' (Logik 257/213).

*Second*, Heidegger maintains that Hegel's dialectic of space makes impossible the *aside-one another* – that is, the *simultaneity* – of the points (Logik 257/213–214). Hegel shows 'dialectically' that such a structure cannot *be* without now-time being involved in it, yet he does not realize that space's 'temporalization' *erases* the 'indifference' characterizing the manyness of points constituting space. 'Hegel puts time together with space in such a way that he . . . removes the "and" between space and time' (Logik 257/214) and thus makes them *indistinguishable*.

*Third*, Heidegger insinuates that one of the reasons 'Hegel is unable to understand the temporal function of time' (Logik 257/213) is that he *begins* from space (Logik 258/215). Understanding time through space *could not but* disclose time as now-time, which is the wrong way to understand time.

## 3 Hegel on Time and the Concept

### 3.1 Introduction

Section 1 has presented early Heidegger's account of time. It consists of two main theses: (a) *time*'s 'originary' nature is 'temporality' and (b) the understanding of *being* is grounded in 'temporality'. Section 2 has reviewed Heidegger's early reading and critique of Hegel's conception of time. It has concluded that Heidegger's view is that, for Hegel, (a) *time*'s 'originary' nature is not temporality but rather now-time and (b) the understanding of *being* is not grounded in temporality but rather in 'the concept' or 'absolute being' (or 'the absolute'), a dimension of which is timelessness (or 'eternity' or 'infinity').

Section 3 will attempt to defend Heidegger's *reading* (but not his *critique*) of Hegel against the objection that Hegel's position is, when all is said and done, identical to Heidegger's (in the sense that both temporalize ontology).[63] For the *objection* to hold, *two* conditions must be satisfied. (a) *First Condition*: It must be shown, contra Heidegger, that, for Hegel, time either covers the Same Domain as 'the concept' (call this *SD*) or has a Higher Ontological Status

[62] The role of 'mattering' in Heidegger's critique of Hegel figures prominently in Pippin (2024). Compare Trisokkas (2024).

[63] As noted, this view was common in Heidegger's time and was raised as a critique of Heidegger; see Williams (1989: 136) and Gadamer (1977: 69, 230). Kojève (1980: 100–149) endorses this view.

than 'the concept' by being a 'ground' or an 'origin' of it (call this *HOS*). (b) *Second Condition*: It must be shown, contra Heidegger, that, for Hegel, time's 'originary' nature is temporality rather than now-time.

On the one hand, if only the First Condition is satisfied, the objection does not hold, for the mode of time that either covers the Same Domain as 'the concept' or has a Higher Ontological Status than 'the concept' *could* be now-time (rather than 'temporality'). In this case, Hegel would indeed be temporalizing ontology but this would have a completely different meaning than Heidegger's temporalization of ontology. On the other hand, if only the Second Condition is satisfied, the objection would once more fail, for temporality could be only a 'moment' of 'the concept' rather than the whole of it or its 'ground'.

I will, first (Sections 3.2–3.4), argue that the First Condition is not satisfied and, therefore, that the objection fails. This entails that Heidegger's reading of Hegel overcomes the objection. I will, second (Section 3.5), (a) present Kojève's argument for the thesis that both conditions are satisfied (and hence that the objection succeeds, which entails that Heidegger's reading of Hegel is false) and (b) show why it fails.

## 3.2 Logos, Eternity, and God in Hegel's System

To determine whether the First Condition is satisfied, namely whether either SD or HOS holds, we must come to grips with Hegel's *system*. In this and the next section, I focus on SD; in Section 3.4, I turn my attention to HOS.

Hegel insists that 'the system' presents 'the whole' and 'the truth'. As he puts it in the *Phenomenology*'s Preface, 'the true shape in which the truth exists can only be the scientific[64] system of it' (PG 14/3). He also writes therein that 'the true is the whole' (PG 24/11). 'The truth' and 'the whole', 'the subject-matter' (*die Sache*) of Hegel's 'system' or 'philosophy', are expressions referring to being's *essential* structure. As Hegel remarks, 'philosophy . . . observes, not the *unessential* determination [of being], but a determination [of it] insofar as it is essential' (PG 46/27). The system (the whole, the truth), though, consists of *three* 'sciences', each presenting a *dimension* of being. Being, *taken as a unity*, has the character of 'the concept' (or 'thought'). The three sciences are logic, philosophy of nature, and philosophy of spirit, and the three ontological dimensions are logos, nature, and spirit.

One could argue *against* SD by showing that, for Hegel, at least one of the three ontological dimensions is not covered by time. Such a case could be made

[64] The terms 'science' and 'scientific' denote a particular *method* in which *philosophical* knowledge is achieved and exhibited. It is characterized by necessary development and immanence (WL I 19/SL 11–12; Enz III §379 Zusatz/6–7). Heidegger reads much more into Hegel's term 'science' than simply a method for knowledge; see Trisokkas (2021).

for logos as expounded by logic. In the *Science of Logic*, Hegel famously writes that 'one can then say that this content [of logic] is the presentation of God, as He is in His eternal essence before the creation of nature and finite spirit' (WL I 44/SL 29, translation modified).

Five points are pertinent here:

*First*, God's essence, which is said to be logic's content, namely logos,[65] is characterized as 'eternal'. There are numerous other passages in the Hegel corpus where logos is described as 'eternal' (*ewig*) or 'eternity' (*Ewigkeit*).[66] So it is undeniable that, for Hegel, there is an ontological dimension covered by eternity.

*Second*, what is presented in logic, God's eternal essence, *logos*, is said to be presented as it is '*before* the creation of nature and finite spirit'. In the system, time emerges in the philosophy of *nature* and hence belongs to the *dimension* of *nature*. If (a) time is a 'natural' element and (b) logos' eternity is *before* nature's creation, eternity is *not* time and hence pure logos is not covered by time. One should be careful here *not* to understand the 'before' temporally. Eternity cannot be said to be 'before' time temporally, as this would be gibberish (Stone 2005: 66). Eternity must be thought without being *opposed* to time. It is *simply* a dimension *grounding* or *enabling* time. If eternity is not to be *opposed* to time, time can only be a 'moment' (not an 'effect' or an absolute 'other') of it, in the sense that it is *formed* by it. It may be said that eternity is the 'diamond net' preventing time from collapsing (cf. Enz II §246 Zusatz/11).

That eternity does not come 'before' time temporally (a nonsensical idea) is asserted forcefully at the beginning of Hegel's *Philosophy of Nature*. It is said there that 'eternity is not before or after time' (Enz II §247 Zusatz/15) and that it is 'absolute timelessness' (Enz II §258 Zusatz/36). Hegel also writes that 'the notion of eternity must not be grasped negatively as abstraction from time, as existing as it were, outside of time; nor in a sense which makes eternity come *after* time, for this would turn eternity into futurity, one of the moments of time' (Enz II §258 Remark/35). 'Eternity', then, signifies neither an opposition to time nor an abstraction from time, *yet it is 'absolute timelessness'*. In my view, Hegel's 'eternity' is simply the 'pure concept' *making time possible*, time's 'transcendental' ground. This is the sense of Hegel's identification of eternity with 'the absolute present' and 'the now, without before or after' (Enz II §247

---

[65] 'For Hegel, ... eternal divinity ... is the very *logos* of the world' (Karpinski 2022: 128).

[66] For example, PG 24/11, 395/325, 396/326, 495/446, 553/460, 559/464–465, 561–562/466–468, 571/476, 581/484; WL I 78, 259/SL 55, 189; WL II 285–286, 490, 492/SL 538, 691, 693; Enz I §19 Zusatz 2/49, §64/113, §86 Zusatz 2/138, §161 Zusatz/235, §213 Zusatz/284, §214 Remark/286; Enz III §379 Zusatz/7.

Zusatz/15). The eternal *is* 'the logical' (the a priori categories), that which prevents nature and spirit from collapsing into nothingness.[67]

This is why Hegel stresses that nature's and spirit's 'creation' from eternity is not a temporal event but rather an *absolute presence*, an event occurring timelessly and 'always'. As he writes, 'the world is created, is now being created, and has eternally been created' (Enz II §247 Zusatz/15). Additionally, in the *Encyclopedia Logic*, he writes, extraordinarily, that 'God not only created a world that as an other stands over against him but also . . . has, *from all eternity*, produced a son in whom he is with himself as spirit' (Enz I §161 Zusatz/235). If God is logos, then Christ (spirit) *is* created by logos, *not at a certain time*, but *from all eternity*, namely endlessly and always.[68]

*Third*, the passage concerns the content of logic, 'logos'. 'God' is a *name* (PG 26/12) Hegel employs to refer to this content. As noted in the *Encyclopedia Logic*,

> only in thinking *and as thinking* is this content, *God Himself*, in its truth. In this sense, then, thought is not just *mere* thought, but rather the highest and, properly viewed, the only manner in which it is possible to comprehend what is eternal and in and for itself. (Enz I §19 Zusatz 2/49).

We should be careful, therefore, not to bring any traditional connotations of 'God' into our understanding of logic. Logic begins with pure, indeterminate being because Hegel wanted to avoid dogmatism regarding the understanding of being, so this 'pure being' cannot *immediately* be determined by means of any of the traditional notions of God. Logic is only about letting *logos* present *itself* as an ontological dimension without any external philosophical, religious, or commonsensical interference.

In the *Phenomenology*'s Preface, Hegel writes that the system's beginning is God, but he quickly adds that the word 'God', posited at the beginning, 'is a meaningless sound, a mere name' (PG 26/12). Still one may ask why God, characterized as 'the eternal' (PG 26/12), is mentioned at all in connection with the system's beginning. Hegel responds that this 'name' is used only insofar as it denotes the enquiry's *subject-matter*. 'God', that is, is used only insofar as it picks out what the system is about: *being* or 'absolute being'.[69] Philosophy's subject-matter is not 'zoology', so it does not start with 'the animal' (PG 23–24/11). Its topic is being and since 'God' paradigmatically refers to being, philosophy may use this word to describe its starting point. Yet nothing more is meant by it than being 'as such'.

---

[67] Williams (1989: 142) explicitly denies this, calling Hegel 'an anti-transcendental philosopher'.

[68] See Welchman (2016: 200) for a similar view.

[69] Hegelian logic begins with *being* precisely because this is 'the subject-matter itself' of philosophy, of 'science as such', taken 'without preliminary reflections' (WL I 35/SL 23, translation modified).

*Fourth*, logic's content, logos or being 'as such', which pervades the other two dimensions of 'absolute being' or 'the concept', nature and spirit, is not something 'subjective', namely something leaving aside or behind an ontological residue, a 'thing in itself'. In the *Phenomenology*, Hegel painstakingly argues that all attempts to begin the enquiry into being with the so-called opposition of consciousness, the distinction between a knowing *subject* and a given *object* that is to be known, fail. This opposition's collapse has provided the 'justification' of Hegel's beginning philosophy (the system) with only its 'subject-matter', namely *being*. Yet, precisely because not only philosophy's 'subject-matter' is *being* but also *thought* itself begins the enquiry into being with the positing of being, the latter provides the starting point of not only being but also the thought of being. Hegelian philosophy, therefore, presents not only the structure of being but also the structure of ontological thought.[70] After all, as Hegel asserts, 'thinking in its immanent determinations, and the true nature of things, are one and the same content' (WL I 38/SL 25).

*Fifth*, the distinction between logic and the other two systematic 'sciences' is confirmed by Hegel's placing philosophy of nature and philosophy of spirit in the sphere of *Realphilosophie* and excluding logic from it (WL I 18/SL 11). *Realphilosophie* is that sphere exhibiting ontological structures occurring in the context of space and time. Since Hegel excludes logic, *considered purely in itself*, from *Realphilosophie*, he *distinguishes* eternity from time. As Surber puts it, 'what is lacking [in logic] is an account of the universal determinations which we employ in encountering *nature* as a realm which is given to us by virtue of the particularizing conditions of space and time' (Surber 1979: 369).

All this leads to the conclusion that, for Hegel, the understanding of being involves eternity. 'Eternity' stands for logical purity, for the pure categories making nature and spirit possible. This is pretty similar to Kant's account of the transcendental categories, with the crucial difference that while for Kant eternity characterizes only a dimension of the human mind, for Hegel eternity characterizes a dimension of being *itself*. While Kant's eternity leaves a residue of being ('the thing in itself') beyond the understanding of being, Hegel's eternity does not leave such a residue.[71]

---

[70] This 'ontological' reading of Hegelian logic contrasts with that 'transcendental' reading taking it to be *only* a presentation of the a priori elements of *our* thought of (empirical) objects, to wit, a project identical to Kant's transcendental logic in the *Critique of Pure Reason*. Houlgate has provided conclusive evidence in support of the 'ontological' reading (Houlgate 2006a: 115–143). The *locus classicus* of the 'transcendental' interpretation is Pippin (1989).

[71] 'Hegel's interpretation is . . . similar to – but more sophisticated than – Kant's conception of the nontemporal eternal, with the crucial exception that for Kant nontemporal things are cognitively

If this conclusion holds, it follows that time does *not* cover the dimension of logos and hence SD fails. This means that Heidegger's reading of Hegel has not been undermined.

## 3.3 Logos, Nature, and Spirit in Hegel's System

### *3.3.1 Logic as a Non-derivative Science*

The conclusion of Section 3.2 can be challenged if one relinquishes the idea that nature and spirit 'derive' (in some non-temporary sense) from pure logos or even that the three dimensions delineated in Hegel's system are equally 'originary' and suggests instead that either nature or spirit (or both taken together) is the ontological dimension from which pure logos derives by means of 'abstraction' from 'the particularizing conditions of space and time'. In this scenario, being is 'originarily' nature or/and spirit ('the concrete concept') and pure logos is an *underdetermined* version of nature or/and spirit ('the abstract concept') (Enz III §377 Zusatz/3). So, although the system develops from logic to philosophy of nature to philosophy of spirit, this development amounts neither to an exposition of three equiprimordial ontological dimensions nor to a development from the most originary dimension to the less originary dimensions but rather to a development from the less originary dimension (the abstract concept) to the more originary dimensions (the concrete concept). Given that (a) both nature and spirit materialize in the framework of time and (b) at least one of them constitutes, ex hypothesi, originary or 'essential' being ('the concept'), SD is validated.

This attempt to support SD fails, mainly for two reasons. *First*, despite certain ambiguous remarks in the Introduction to the *Philosophy of Spirit* (Enz III §377/3, §377 Zusatz/3, §384 Remark/18), there is evidence that Hegel considers logic a *non-derivative* 'science' that is *at least as 'originary'* as the other two systematic 'sciences'. For example, Hegel characterizes 'metaphysics', what his 'logic' is about, the 'holy of holies' (WL I 14/SL 8) and writes that it is '*just as* remarkable . . . when a people loses its metaphysics' as when it loses its interest in science, morality, politics, and so on (i.e. its interest in the issues pertaining to philosophy of nature and philosophy of spirit) (WL I 13/SL 7, my emphasis). He stresses that each 'particular' concept, including the concept of *spirit* (and, we should add, the concept of *nature*), 'derives from . . . the logical idea' and is 'a necessary development of the eternal idea' (Enz III §379 Zusatz/6–7). It seems, therefore, that logic, the 'science' presenting 'the concept' in its purity or 'eternity', is at least as 'originary' as the *Realphilosophie*.

inaccessible. For Kant, nontemporality only achieves significance in relation to practical concerns, that is, in relation to freedom. For Hegel such a limitation does not appear' (Welchman 2016: 199).

*Second*, if (a) pure logos is an 'abstraction' *from* nature or/and spirit, which ex hypothesi is/are 'originary' being, and (b) eternity determines pure logos, then eternity must be present in 'originary' being. To 'abstract' *x* from *y* means to isolate *x* from all other elements being present in *y*. This entails that *x* is *already* present in *y*. Therefore, the objection presupposes that eternity is already present in nature or/and spirit. There are passages in Hegel's text suggesting that pure logos is hidden in natural and spiritual structures. He writes that the *pure*, *eternal* categories are hidden in 'human language' and that they pervade 'everything that in some way or other has become for [man] a representation' (WL I 20/SL 12; see also Stein 2021: 271). They permeate nature and the empirical sciences, for they 'operate in the medium of the most common categories (e.g. whole and parts, a thing and its properties, and the like)' (WL I 21/SL 13). Hegel writes that 'nature is the idea' (Enz II §247 Zusatz/15) and has 'eternal life' in it (Enz II §252 Zusatz/27). Moreover, he explicitly states that 'history . . . is ruled by divine providence' – that is, by *logos* (Enz III §377 Zusatz/4) – and that 'spirit is the infinite idea' (Enz III §386/22).

Nevertheless, even if pure logos' presence in nature or/and spirit suffices for rejecting the objection, it is clear that Hegel does not regard pure logos as an 'abstraction' from nature or/and spirit. We saw him explicitly stating that 'the notion of eternity must not be grasped . . . as abstraction from time' (Enz II §258 Remark/35). Hegel rejects the *process* of 'abstraction' because of his view concerning the *beginning* of the understanding of being, namely that being cannot be understood if one *begins* from nature or/and spirit. The sole beginning of ontology is pure, indeterminate being, whose development generates the sphere of pure logos, the a priori categories of thought and being.

Given these two reasons, SD must be rejected. Such a rejection strengthens the view that Heidegger reads Hegel correctly when he claims that, for Hegel, time is *not* the sole ground of ontology. Of course, the simple affirmation of eternity's presence in a three-dimensional 'absolute being' ('the absolute', 'the concept') does not specify the exact relation between these dimensions. Let me, then, briefly look at this relation.

### 3.3.2 Eternity and Time in Hegel's System

Hegel's 'system' or 'philosophy', which presents 'absolute being' or 'the concept',[72] contains both eternity and time. Eternity defines logos in its purity and time defines logos in its naturalized and spiritualized manifestations. Naturalized and spiritualized logos is pure logos that has been 'realized' or, if you like, become 'real' in space and time (hence Hegel's calling of the 'philosophical sciences' that present this manifestation of logos *Realphilosophien*).

[72] 'It is the task of philosophy to grasp . . . the concept' (Enz III §384 Remark/18).

Pure logos' becoming 'real', though, does not cancel eternity out – it only gives it a content that it does not have when one considers it only logically. Consequently, since nature and spirit are determined by time, time is not therein opposed to eternity as its absolute other, as what is devoid of eternity. In the manifestations of naturalized and spiritualized logos, in other words, one finds eternity in time. Yet this presence of eternity in time entails neither the reduction of eternity to time nor the reduction of time to eternity. They remain *distinct* in 'the absolute' despite that presence.

On the one hand, 'the concept' or 'the absolute' is *never solely* eternity. This would be 'only a dead, empty abstraction' (Enz III §386 Zusatz/24). For Hegel, God (pure logos) never existed alone and *only then* created nature and spirit. Hegel's system does not accommodate *transcendence* (in the Kantian, not the Heideggerian sense). God, *pure logos*, logos qua logos, *is* an *immanent* element *pervading nature and spirit*. On the other hand, though, 'the concept' can *never* be *solely* time. Despite being immanent, pure logos is not *reduced* to nature and/or spirit. For Hegel, nature and/or spirit (history) never existed alone and only then, somehow, generated eternity (as a 'mathematical', 'biological', or a 'cultural' 'idea'). *Hegel is neither a naturalist nor a historicist.* As an interpreter perfectly puts it, 'Hegel is not . . . beginning with our sense of time and attempting to 'fit' God into it' (Karpinski 2022: 136). (Yet Hegel is also *not* a 'logicist', in the sense that he reduces nature and spirit to logos.)

Even though pure logos, nature, and spirit can never be *separated* in 'the concept', crucially the *understanding* of being cannot *begin* from nature or spirit (i.e. from time). This holds because if this were to happen, logos, eternity, God, infinity would be seen as *products of time, man, finitude*, rather than as what they really are, namely, genuine expressions of timelessness (cf. OHU 299). Moreover, even though the three dimensions cannot be separated in 'the concept', pure logos is, one may say, the 'ground' of the other two, in the very specific sense that it facilitates their formation. Precisely because only pure logos is the 'ground', the time of nature and spirit is only 'a copy of the eternal idea' (Enz III §377 Zusatz/24). Eternity, logical form, has indeed a presence in nature and spirit, yet it is always manifested through structures involving intuition/matter and defined by spatio-temporality. These are the structures Hegel calls 'finite beings' or simply 'finitude' (Enz III §386 Zusatz/24). It is exactly this involvement that, as in Plato, makes time *only* a *copy* of eternity and that, ultimately, manifests it as now-time, *eternity qua succession* (which is, as Heidegger puts it, a 'vulgar' conception of eternity).

### 3.3.3 The Transition from Logic to Philosophy of Nature

Crucial for understanding the relation between eternity and time in Hegel's system is the 'transition' (a) from logic (pure logos) to philosophy of nature (naturalized logos) and (b) from philosophy of nature (naturalized logos) to philosophy of spirit (spiritualized logos). Hegelian logic culminates in 'the absolute idea', which determines *being* (WL II 549, 551, 572/SL 735, 736, 752; Trisokkas 2022b: 351–353) as *self-determined* pure logos (Houlgate 2005: 106–108). As self-determined pure logos, the absolute idea contains all the categories of thought and being disclosed in logic. It is the pure concept generating the totality of its determinations. Yet the absolute idea cannot *just* be a totality. It is also a *single* posited determination. As posited, the absolute idea is, as Hegel puts it, a '*simple relation to itself*' (*einfache Beziehung auf sich*) (WL II 572/SL 752, translation modified). It simply *is*. So, logically, the absolute idea (the totality of being's logical determinations) necessarily 'collect[s] itself in the immediacy of *being*' (WL II 573/SL 752).[73]

This 'immediacy of being' in which the totality of pure logos results is posited as *nature* (WL II 573/SL 752). Nature, therefore, is simply the absolute idea that has folded into itself and become immediate. Since nature *is* the absolute idea, it contains pure logos: it is *pervaded* by the categories. As Hegel puts it, 'there is no transition that takes place; the simple being to which the idea determines itself remains perfectly transparent to it: it is the idea that in its determination remains with itself' (SL 752–753).

Yet nature is not only pure logos; it is *also* what is *not* logical, for while pure logos *is* the *self-determined* totality of categories, nature is *immediate* being. By being immediate *rather than self-determined*, nature is pure logos' *opposite*.[74] As Hegel has it, by becoming nature, pure logos has proven to be 'the negative of itself' (Enz II §247/13). By losing its character of self-determination, pure logos becomes 'externality' or 'asunderness' (Enz II §247/13). This means that nature is indeed 'formed' by the categories, yet it also involves what is non-categorial, non-logical, non-conceptual, namely intuition.[75] Recall that Hegel emphasizes not only the logical but also the intuitive aspect of space and time

[73] Note that *this* immediate being is *not* the repositing of the immediate being with which the logic started. In contrast to the latter, the absolute idea is the immediate being *of the totality of pure determinations*.

[74] 'The ideas with which the logic terminates posit the whole of (material) nature as their antithesis' (Welchman 2016: 197).

[75] It is difficult to specify exactly what Hegel means by 'intuition' and such a specification is beyond the scope of this Element. For my purposes, it suffices only that it is undeniable that nature and spirit are not merely pure logos and that the difference is facilitated by means of the aspect of intuition. For an attempt to specify the exact meaning of 'intuition' in Hegel's philosophy of nature, see Kaufmann et al. (2021).

(Enz II §258 Remark/34; WL II 535/SL 724), which provide the basic framework of all nature (Kaufmann et al. (2021)).

What matters to us here is solely that Hegel explains the 'transition' from eternity (pure logos) to time (nature) in such a way that eternity is not annihilated. Even though time is distinct from eternity, they are not *separated*; they rather mesh into a *unity*. This is the meaning of the 'transition' from logic to philosophy of nature.

### 3.3.4 The Transition from Philosophy of Nature to Philosophy of Spirit

Regarding the 'transition' from nature to spirit, Hegel's focus is the determination of an *aspect* of the relation between logos and nature that cannot fit into the context of immediate being and asunderness characterizing nature. This aspect is *self-consciousness* and the *freedom* ensuing from it. Philosophy of nature expounds what becomes of the categories as they pervade nature and form intuition/matter. Logos is *not* conscious of *itself* in its simple formation of *nature*.[76]

As spirit, logos acquires a variety of structures which function towards *logos' becoming conscious of itself in nature*, namely becoming conscious of itself while being embodied and being surrounded by other bodies and being involved in practices (ranging from habitual practices, such as loving and loathing, to more advanced ones, such as voting, painting, worshipping, and doing philosophy). When nature arrives at that situation in which the conditions are ripe for the emergence of logos' self-consciousness, nature is transformed into spirit.[77] Philosophy of spirit expounds the various ways in which logos gradually comes to find *itself* in *nature* and thereby becomes 'free', to wit, without any opposition (Enz III §386/22). It is exactly these structures of the gradual self-finding of logos in nature that Hegel calls 'spirit': 'All activity of spirit is … only an apprehension of itself, and the aim of all genuine science is just this, that spirit shall recognize itself in everything in heaven and on earth. There is simply no out-and-out Other for spirit' (Enz III §377, Zusatz/3).

As with the 'transition' from logos to nature, the 'transition' from nature to spirit does not cancel that from which the 'transition' is made. For Hegel, spirit is not a transcendent being that at some temporal moment attaches itself to nature. It is, rather, irrevocably connected with nature from the beginning and

[76] Enz II §247 Zusatz/14 (translation modified): 'Nature is the Idea, but only in itself'; Enz III §577/276: 'Nature [is] the process of the Idea that is *in itself*.'

[77] 'Consciousness is where organic nature acquires its highest point of concentration by reflecting upon itself and where nature as such thus becomes spirit' (Di Giovanni 2010: xix).

always.[78] Spiritualized logos is always already naturalized logos (as it is always already pure logos). As Nuzzo puts it, 'while nature is indeed "sublated" in and by *Geist*, it is never entirely left behind in the articulation of spirit's reality' (Nuzzo 2013: 1). *Logos*' first attempt to find *itself* in nature manifests itself as the animal's *embodied* soul, yet this gradually develops into the distinctively human self-consciousness and the objective ways in which it manifests itself in nature (such as property and the state). Philosophy of spirit culminates in 'the absolute spirit', the highest form of which is (doing) *philosophy*. 'Philosophy' is nothing but the realization of embodied finite spirit (man) that being cannot be *understood* unless pure logos, 'the absolutely universal', posits nature as its other and then, as spirit, 'sublates' this otherness by becoming conscious of itself in nature (Enz III §577/276). In this way, the whole system comes full circle, necessitating thus a new beginning of the process leading from logic to philosophy of nature to philosophy of spirit.

An array of details must, of course, be disclosed if the relation between nature and spirit is to be understood in a non-formulaic, non-simplistic fashion. Yet this is not our concern here. For our purposes, it suffices to notice that, for Hegel, spirit always has a natural and hence temporal dimension. Spirit strives to find itself in nature, not from a point of view beyond nature, but rather while being always already fully connected to nature. Spirit, then, for Hegel, is always already in nature and hence 'in time'. It *differs* from nature, though, since it is not simply the immediate being, the self-externality, of pure logos, but rather it is logos that strives to find (i.e. to become conscious of) *itself* in that immediate being. Yet, spirit, qua finite spirit, differs also from pure logos,[79] for it strives to find itself *in nature*, while logos qua logos is the simple or 'comparatively abstract' exposition of the categories (Enz III §377 Zusatz/3), the self-determination of the absolute idea, the 'eternal essence [of God] before the creation of nature and of a finite spirit' (WL I 44/SL 29).

All in all, what I have tried to show in the whole of Section 3.3 is that it is impossible to remove any of the three dimensions of 'absolute being' or 'the absolute' or 'the concept' in Hegel's system without the whole system collapsing. *None* of the three dimensions is *reduced* to any of the others. If this is combined with the fact that pure logos, the self-determined totality of the *pure* categories of thought and being, is (a) described as 'eternal' and (b) distinguished from nature and spirit (the *Realphilosophien*) precisely in that while

[78] As Nuzzo (2013: 2, my emphasis) correctly notes, the embodied spirit 'remains the *permanent* basis of spirit's development'. As she, again correctly, puts it, nature is 'constitutive' of spirit and spirit relates 'immanently' to nature (Nuzzo 2013: 4).

[79] One of the first to acknowledge the distinction between logos and spirit was Hartmann (1957: 216).

they are in time, it is not, we can conclude that time does *not* cover the whole domain of being or 'the concept'. This suffices for rejecting SD and thereby validating Heidegger's reading of Hegel.

## 3.4 Time in the *Phenomenology*

Let us now turn to HOS, the thesis that, for Hegel, time has a Higher Ontological Status than 'the concept' or 'the absolute' by being a 'ground' or an 'origin' of it (see Section 3.1). Even if SD fails, for the reason that time is only one dimension of 'the concept' (see Section 3.3), Heidegger's claim that, for Hegel, time is *not* ontology's sole ground would still be undermined if HOS held. This is so because in this case 'the concept', namely the whole of Hegel's system, would be grounded in a kind of time that has a presence 'before' the system, that is 'presupposed' by the system.

The examination of HOS requires a discussion of the relation between Hegel's *phenomenology* and his system.[80] This is so because Hegel himself characterizes phenomenology as the system's 'justification' (WL I 42/SL 28) and 'presupposition' (WL I 43/SL 29). Since phenomenology concerns *spirit*, which materializes in *time*, it could be said that the relation between phenomenology and the system establishes HOS.

Yet, for HOS to be established, it must *follow* from phenomenology's 'justificatory' function that its domain, which is indeed 'in time' (since it involves spirit), is *ontological*, to wit, that it discloses, not a phenomenal or erroneous understanding of being, but, rather, a truth about being. In short, it must tell us something truthful about being, even if this will not be said in terms of 'the concept' or 'the system'. If this held, one would be justified to claim that 'the concept' derives from a truth, an ontological understanding that is fundamentally determined by time, that is more 'originary' than it. This would mean that the kind of time delimiting the phenomenological framework, 'historical time', is more 'originary' than that dimension of 'the concept' in which time 'disappears', namely pure logos. It would mean that timelessness (logic) is posited *through* time (phenomenology). This would historicize or 'spiritualize' pure logos and timelessness; it would make them a product of 'finite spirit' or 'the subject', man (Enz III §377/3), considered as the entity thinking and acting in a historical 'world'. They would just be a 'cultural' product, an 'idea' the historical human brain and praxis have *constructed*.

There are many interpretations of the *Phenomenology* and some do read it as presenting 'truth as a historical process of disclosure of being' (Williams 1989: 141), as a 'pre-categorial ontology' that logic 'presupposes' (Aschenberg 1976:

[80] By contrast, the discussion of SD concerned only Hegel's system.

220–221). There are also interpretations *denying* that Hegelian phenomenology makes a *positive* contribution to the understanding of being. Winfield and Houlgate, for example, regard phenomenology as Hegel's intricate argument for rejecting the thesis that philosophy must begin its enquiry into being with given determinations or 'presuppositions' (Winfield 2013: 1–29; Houlgate 2005: 26–66, 101–105; 2006a: 144–162; see also Trisokkas 2012: 71–92; 2021: 132–136). Phenomenology, for them, has a predominantly negative character and its purpose is only to argue *against* the suggestion that the *beginning* of ontology depends upon the spatio-temporal world. This, of course, does not entail that the spatio-temporal world won't be shown to contribute positively to the understanding of being farther down the road. This will indeed be the case in philosophy of nature and philosophy of spirit. But as concerns its *beginning*, the enquiry into the understanding of being does not depend upon this world. For Winfield and Houlgate, the system is grounded in or justified by phenomenology *only* in the sense that phenomenology removes the possibility of beginning philosophy in any other way than with pure, indeterminate being. It removes this possibility by showing how 'consciousness', the attempt to achieve understanding of being through presuppositions, is led by itself to its total collapse. Thus, as Winfield and Houlgate see it, phenomenology does not disclose a truth, a dimension of *being* that is more 'originary' than pure logos, namely historical time and man's journey through it, but rather it *frees* 'the concept' from historical time so that it can be posited, as pure, indeterminate being, presuppositionlessly.

There are at least three reasons phenomenology's negative interpretation is superior to its positive, ontological interpretation. *First*, Hegel describes consciousness' journey (PG 72/49) in the phenomenological domain as 'a self-completing scepticism' (*sich vollbringende Skeptizismus*) (PG 72/50, translation modified) and as 'the pathway of *doubt*, or more precisely as the way of despair' (PG 72/49). Such characterizations suggest that the phenomenology describes *erroneous* attempts by finite spirit (man) to begin the enquiry into the understanding of being. Indeed, Hegel writes that 'the determinations that constitute the nature of . . . phenomenal consciousness . . . block the entrance to philosophy [and] they are the errors that must be removed before one can enter it' (WL I 37–38/SL 25).

*Second*, the beginning of Hegelian logic is preceded by an 'external' reflection on how the understanding of being should begin (WL I 65–87/SL 45–57). This reflection concludes that the *only* possible beginning of such an understanding is pure, indeterminate being. This suggests that phenomenology, being located outside the system and beginning with the sensible given, does not express a positive understanding of being. It only 'clears the way' for such an understanding to begin. This is why Hegel writes that '[at] the beginning of logic . . . there is only present the resolve, which can also be viewed as arbitrary, of considering *thinking as such*', which, precisely because it does not carry any presuppositions, is nothing but '*pure being*' (WL I 68/SL 48).

*Third*, Hegel describes the dialectic of each 'form of consciousness' in phenomenology as culminating in 'our' realization that its 'experience' (i.e. the *undermining* of its constitutive beliefs) would not have been possible unless certain a priori concepts, unbeknownst to it, had *already* been at work in it.[81] It is this realization that each time forces the 'transition' to a new form of consciousness. These a priori concepts are the 'categories' that logic will deduce in an orderly fashion from pure, indeterminate being, to wit, from sheer presuppositionlessness (WL I 17/SL 10). Surber writes that in phenomenology 'experience . . . discover[s] that it contains in itself and is permeated through and through by the universality of the true content of science' (Surber 1979: 368) and Harris remarks that the *Phenomenology* shows the 'experience' of consciousness as depending upon 'the conceptual structure of pure science' (Harris 1997: 7), a structure that has the character of 'eternity' (131). This suggests that even though in phenomenology 'consciousness' is occupied with 'the world's' spatio-temporal – including, 'existential' and 'historical' (Heinrichs 1974: xiii) – 'data', its 'experience' discloses an 'originary' understanding of being that the occupation with those 'data' had hidden. In this way, phenomenology not only does *not* show that the beginning of the system depends upon historical time but also proves that historical time has *already* been pervaded by logos and eternity.

Given these reasons, I conclude that HOS fails and therefore that Heidegger's reading of Hegel cannot be undermined through it. The *Phenomenology* does *not* show that 'historical time' is more 'originary' than pure logos' timelessness. It does *not* show that phenomenological time 'generates' pure logos, that timelessness is posited *through* time. All it shows is that the *beginning* of the understanding of being *cannot* be made with 'historical time' or 'temporality'.

## 3.5 Kojève on the Identity of Time and the Concept

### *3.5.1 Rejection of Kojève's Textual Evidence*

A reading of Hegel which sought to *affirm* both SD and HOS and exercised immense influence on Hegel scholarship, especially in France (Tegos 2023: 15–34), is Alexandre Kojève's, as presented in his text 'A Note on Eternity, Time, and the Concept' (1938–9) (Kojève 1980). Kojève's reading is the opposite of Heidegger's.

[81] Hegel writes that '[*we*] recognize (*erkennen*) the pure concepts of science in this form of shapes of consciousness' (PG 491/589). For a detailed examination of this idea see Heinrichs (1974). See also Houlgate (2013: 8–13).

While the latter claims that (a) 'the concept' is, for Hegel, more originary than time and (b) Hegel's conception of time is the 'vulgar' conception, Kojève maintains that (a) 'the concept',[82] for Hegel, is identified with time (Kojève 1980: 102) and (b) Hegel's conception of time not only is distinct from the 'vulgar' conception but also is very close to that conception which takes time to be 'existential-ontological' 'temporality' (Kojève 1980: 130–131, 133).[83] Kojève attempts to support this twofold claim with both textual evidence and philosophical reasons.

The textual evidence Kojève provides in support of his claim is, however, weak. He employs *exclusively* Hegel's statement in the *Phenomenology* that '*time* is the *concept* itself which *is there*' (PG 584/487; see also PG 45–46/27; Kojève 1980: 101, 131–132). Kojève thinks that what this excerpt says is that the concept is *nothing but* time or that the concept is *only* temporal.[84] But it does not say this. Hegel's assertion says something about time, yet it does not say anything about the concept *in its entirety*. Time is the concept itself 'which is there', which is disclosed 'empirically' (Kojève 1980: 132), but this does *not* mean that *the whole concept* ('the system' or 'the whole'), the concept in the totality of its 'ways', is time. The excerpt allows the interpretation that the concept, even though it is indeed time, is *also* 'eternity', which Kojève himself defines as 'nontemporal reality' and 'something essentially other than time' (Kojève 1980: 101, 103–104), namely *timelessness*. Kojève's thesis, therefore, is not really supported with unequivocal textual evidence.

### 3.5.2 Hegel Between the Parmenideans-Spinozists and the 'Relavitists'

Given the weak textual evidence Kojève offers in support of his claim, I will focus on the philosophical reasons he provides. What drives his argument is the attempt to distinguish Hegel's position from the Parmenidean–Spinozist identification of the concept with eternity, on the one hand, and the 'relative' theses of Plato, Aristotle, and Kant, on the other hand (Kojève 1980: 101, 130–131). For all the latter, Kojève asserts, the concept is 'eternal'[85] and 'possessed by' man,

[82] 'We can call the coherent whole of conceptual understanding that lays claim to the truth – *Begriff*, Concept' and '[we can say that] *the* Concept . . . is the integration of all concepts, the complete system of concepts' (Kojève 1980: 100–101).

[83] This is why Kojève puts Heidegger and Hegel together under the rubric of 'true' philosophy (Kojève 1980: 102, n. 1).

[84] Welchman remarks that Hegel's statement was understood by most to 'suggest a radical attempt to immerse philosophical thought in time' and that 'the famous developmental structures of Hegelian thought represent historicized versions of Kant's categories, plunging concepts into time and history' (Welchman 2016: 195). It would not be an exaggeration to say that the same erroneous view about Hegel still reigns supreme today.

[85] Kojève distinguishes between 'Eternity' and 'eternal'. By being 'eternal', the concept 'participates' in Eternity and 'is an eternal function of Eternity', yet it is 'something other than' Eternity (Kojève 1980: 102).

but *relates* either to an eternity that is outside of time (Plato) or to an eternity that is in time (Aristotle) or to time (Kant) (Kojève 1980: 103–104, 125, 131). By *identifying* the concept with *time*, Hegel avoids both the Parmenidean–Spinozist thesis and the relative thesis (in any of its forms). Kojève strives to distinguish Hegel's position from not only the Parmenidean–Spinozist thesis but also the relative thesis because he thinks that both of them encounter 'difficulties' (Kojève 1980: 131), making them incapable of respecting the *fact* of man's 'historicity' (Kojève 1980: 132–133).

*On the one hand*, Parmenides and Spinoza identify the concept with eternity (Kojève 1980: 102), but they place it outside of man, *precisely because* man is a finite, 'historical' being. As a being not possessing the concept, man could not have *knowledge*, for knowledge can be achieved only through the concept. Yet Parmenides and Spinoza maintain that they express the truth and hence that they have knowledge (Kojève 1980: 118). Consequently, Kojève writes, their position is 'absurd' and they behave as 'mad' men (Kojève 1980: 118–119). If they were consistent, they would remain *silent*: they would not make any claim to knowledge.

*On the other hand*, Plato, Aristotle and Kant place the concept in man, but they characterize it as 'eternal' and *relate* it to something that is distinct from it (Kojève 1980: 103). The problem here is the characterization of the concept, which is possessed by an 'empirical', 'real', 'finite', 'historical', 'non-eternal' being (*man*), as *eternal* (Kojève 1980: 103, 131). Even though the 'relative' account of the concept improves upon the Parmenidean–Spinozist one, since it places it explicitly inside man and hence it does not cancel immediately the possibility of knowledge, it creates the paradox that a temporal and historical being thinks by means of an element which is *not* in time and history.[86] Man 'needs time in order to think by means of the Concept' (Kojève 1980: 118) and yet the concept is said to be outside time.

Kojève claims that, since both the Parmenidean–Spinozist and the 'relative' position cannot explain temporal-historical man's connection with the concept, the *only* way remaining for such an explanation is to identify the concept with time and place it inside man (Kojève 1980: 131). Since human thought and language are temporally and historically determined, the concept must be identified with 'historical time', namely 'the Time in which human history unfolds, or better still, the Time that realizes itself (not as the motion of the stars, for example, but) as universal History' (Kojève 1980: 133).

[86] The paradox of the 'relative' position is that '*concepts*, and consequently *the* integral Concept, subsist in *time*, while being by definition *eternal* – i.e., something essentially other than time' (Kojève 1980: 103–104).

For Kojève, then, the time with which the concept is identified is, in Hegel, *only* historical time, time as it pertains to 'spiritual' man's 'being in the world'; it is not natural (or 'cosmic') time (Kojève 1980: 134, 136). Thus Kojève's interpretation of Hegel's conception of time is the opposite of Heidegger's, who, as seen, claims that, for Hegel, time is, first and foremost, natural time. As explained, Heidegger thinks that, for Hegel, historical time is only the 'filling' of natural (mathematical) time with man's practical and sociopolitical activity (see Section 2). In fact, Kojève, as soon as he identifies Hegelian time with historical time, continues by describing it in terms that bring it very close to Heidegger's 'temporality'. He writes that, for Hegel, time 'does not exist outside of Man', that 'Time *is* Man', and that 'Time is characterized by the primacy of the Future' (Kojève 1980: 134). Thus, he tells us, Hegel is opposed to pre-Hegelian philosophy, which conceived time as 'cosmic' time, as being outside of man and having a mathematical nature, and gave priority to the present (Kojève 1980: 134). In historical time, the future has priority, because man, in whose constitution time belongs, is determined fundamentally by what Kojève calls 'the Project' (Kojève 1980: 134, n. 21). This is another name for Heidegger's 'projection'[87] and denotes Dasein's openness to acting towards the realization of its possibilities (Kojève 1980: 136) (see Section 1).

What Kojève has failed to notice is that Hegel's position can be distinguished from Kojève's two constructed poles *also* by taking the concept to be *not only* time *but also* eternity (timelessness). Such a position does not imply *transcendence*, for the concept does not *relate* to anything; it is not a relatum.[88] The concept *is* eternity (as the Parmenidean–Spinozist position declares) and *is* time (as Kojève claims). It *is* also possessed by man (as 'the relativists' assert).

Kojève assumes that Hegel did not make the 'absurd' or 'mad' claim that the temporal-historical man thinks eternity by means of the eternal concept. Yet this

---

[87] For Kojève's relation to Heidegger see Tegos (2023). Kojève discusses 'the Project' in relation to the analysis of *desire* in Hegel's *Phenomenology* (Kojève 1980: 134ff.; see also Tazi 2018). This discussion, however, neither is relevant to my present concerns nor undermines in any way my critique of Kojève. The emphasis Kojève gives to desire is another sign of his unbalanced reading of Hegel and the excessive emphasis he puts on the *Phenomenology*. Indeed, as is well known, the French school of Hegel interpretation mistakenly took the *Phenomenology* to be *the* locus of Hegelian philosophy.

[88] Karpinski thinks that because in Hegel eternity is *omnipresent*, it is *transcendent* (Karpinski 2022: 133). This is not a valid inference (Houlgate 2005: 108). Kojève asserts that 'for [Hegel], . . . the Concept is *related* to nothing, except to itself' (Kojève 1980: 104), but he seems to think, as Karpinski does, that if the concept were identified with eternity, it would be transcendent. For him, transcendence is avoided only if the concept is identified with time. This is clearly a mistake, for the concept, precisely because it is non-relational, is 'immanent', not 'transcendent'. Moreover, the non-relational concept can have God (logos, the categories) as one of its dimensions without being transcendent. The Hegelian concept is 'immanent', but not 'atheistic' (cf. Kojève 1980: 106, n. 3).

claim is 'absurd' or 'mad' only if one believes that man is *exclusively* temporal-historical. Hegel disagrees with this belief. Man is temporal-historical only *insofar* as it is a natural being and a finite spirit, but it is not temporal-historical *insofar* as it is logos. For Hegel, 'the absolute', to which everything belongs, including man, is the 'originary' *unity* of logos, nature, and spirit, and each dimension, *while remaining distinct*, meshes with the others.

The 'insofar' or 'qua' is crucial in Hegelian ontology. Qua logos, man can think independently of time, even if the *presentation* (*Darstellung*) of this thinking occurs only 'in time' and thus necessarily has the form of a succession of thoughts. For example, we can think of a static circle, eternity's symbol, even if our thoughts succeed one another in time.[89]

Kojève claims that 'the philosophers who do not identify the Concept and Time cannot give an account of History' (132), for history is fundamentally temporal and the concept cannot grasp time unless it is itself determined by time. How can something that is beyond time be of any use to an understanding of something that is fundamentally determined by time? This statement is problematic, though, since an account of history can be given even if only one dimension of the concept is identified with time. The concept *is* time, but also it is *not* time (logos qua logos, i.e. *pure* logos). This is possible because the concept has many dimensions, one of which is eternity (and time is another). This, of course, ascribes a contradictory structure to the concept, yet contradiction is affirmed by Hegel as the structure of 'the truth' or 'the absolute' (WL II 74–75/381–382, 563/745; see also Trisokkas 2016).

### 3.5.3 Why the 'Dimensionalist' Interpretation Is Preferable to Kojève's

I have argued that Kojève's reading of Hegel is undermined on the basis not only of textual evidence but also of philosophical reasoning. Kojève's main idea is that it would be 'mad' to claim that man, being a temporal-historical being, can have access to eternity (Kojève 1980: 119). Yet, if man consists *also* of pure logos, man's existence is not exclusively temporal-historical and hence man *can* access eternity. Kojève could deny that, for Hegel, pure logos is a constituent of man, but in this case he would have to explain logic's presence in the system and, especially, its 'grounding' of the philosophy of (finite) spirit. He does not, though, offer such an explanation and this is, ultimately, why the 'dimensionalist' interpretation is preferable to his. Kojève seems to want to understand the

[89] As Di Giovanni puts it, 'an absolute content which is already at hand in historically conditioned materials ... would [once brought to light] stand on its own without the need of historical support' (Di Giovanni 2010: xvi). See also Hegel's description of the Bacchanalian revel as 'a state of repose' (PG 46 /27–28).

Hegelian system by considering only the realm of spirit and ignoring the system's other parts.[90]

Kojève admits that in philosophy of nature Hegel presents time in non-historical terms, as a natural phenomenon (Kojève 1980: 133). He insists, though, that, for Hegel, what is presented in the philosophy of nature as natural time is 'identified' *at the end* with historical time (Kojève 1980: 133). This 'ultimate' identification, according to Kojève, must be understood as meaning that, for Hegel, 'there is no natural, cosmic Time; there is Time only to the extent that there is *History*, that is, human existence' (Kojève 1980: 133). But if the account of time as natural time in philosophy of nature was to be cancelled out with the arrival of philosophy of spirit, one wonders why it was offered in the first place. Moreover, such an interpretation makes the immanent and necessary 'transition' of logos ('the absolute idea') into *nature* a mere whim.[91]

The 'dimensionalist' reading must explain in detail how the concept's three dimensions (logos, nature, spirit) interrelate in such a way that the concept ('the absolute') can be said to have no relation to anything outside itself. Such an explanation may prove impossible. Nevertheless, such an impossibility does not make Kojève's interpretation correct, as the need remains to give an account of the presence of pure logos, as the ontological dimension that is independent of time, in the Hegelian system.

By identifying the concept with time, Kojève makes the concept dependent upon intuition and matter (what he calls 'empirical existence') (Kojève 1980: 103),[92] which are the elements distinguishing the 'logische' from the 'realphilosophische' domain. By not identifying the concept with time, the 'dimensionalist' interpretation makes a dimension of the concept independent of intuition and matter and hence allows the positing of a domain of purity and logical categories *in being*.

### 3.5.4 Kojève, Heidegger and Hegel on Man

The main objection to Kojève is that he assumes that, for Hegel, man is solely a historical, temporalized being and, therefore, that man can understand being only through time. Heidegger differs from Kojève in that he repudiates this

---

[90] This is reflected in Kojève's declaration that 'the aim of Hegel's philosophy is to give an account of the fact of History' (Kojève 1980: 133). For the 'dimensionalist' interpretation, the aim of Hegel's philosophy is to give an account of 'the absolute'.

[91] It is surreal that Kojève accuses Hegel of not realizing that there cannot be just historical time, that the explanation of 'life' requires 'cosmic or physical Time' (Kojève 1980: 133, n. 20)! But this is exactly what Hegel offers: a 'cosmic or physical time' that 'transforms' into 'historical time' *without itself being annulled*.

[92] Kojève clearly *identifies* time with 'the existence of Man in the world' (Kojève 1980: 104). Eternity, as exhibited in Hegelian logic, does not have this feature.

assumption, recognizing that, for Hegel, man is pervaded by pure logos, which, in Hegel's system, enables man to understand being also 'from timelessness'. Yet Heidegger agrees with Kojève that the claim that being can be understood 'from timelessness' or 'from eternity' is 'absurd' or 'mad', exactly because, as both Heidegger and Kojève assert, man's essence is temporality or finitude. This is the heart of Heidegger's *critique* of Hegel.

We saw (Section 2.7.1) that in *The Concept of Time*, Heidegger objects to Hegel's idea that being can be understood 'from eternity' on the basis that we cannot *begin* 'from eternity'. The 'departure' 'from eternity' is not and can never be 'at our disposal'. Alweiss (2002) takes issue with this claim. She argues that Heidegger's *agreement* with Lévinas and Blanchot that death or non-being is never at our disposal *too* (SZ 250/293–294, 261/305) is fatal to his argument (Alweiss 2002: 126–127). For if the reason we cannot understand being 'from eternity' is that eternity is *never at our disposal*, the same should be said about the understanding 'from temporality/finitude', given that death is *never at our disposal* either. Alweiss points out, though, that Heidegger claims only that what we have at our disposal is death's *certainty*. It is thus that death functions as 'the horizon of possibility' (Alweiss 2002: 126). Yet this is also problematic for Heidegger's argument. Heidegger's claim seems to be that although we are always in being, we can be certain of non-being and that *this suffices for asserting that our departure can be only 'from temporality/finitude'*. This would hold, though, only if (a) we can be certain of non-being *but* (b) *we cannot be certain of eternity or timelessness*. Yet if Heidegger accepts that we can be certain of *non-being*, even though we are always in *being*, it is difficult to see how he could justify the *rejection* of the claim that we can be certain of *timelessness* even though we are always in *time*. To be sure, Hegel was *certain* that timelessness is a dimension of 'the absolute'!

## 3.6 Conclusion

What is problematic in Kojève's interpretation of Hegel, as well as in any other interpretation that considers Hegel's philosophy to be a philosophy that regards man's historicity and hence human, historical time as the sole ontological ground, is its neglect of Hegel's central idea that 'the truth' has the form of the *system*.[93] Spirit, as the dimension in which history materializes, is not but a *part* of the

[93] Karpinski correctly labels the 'popular understanding of Hegel as a philosopher of purely *historical* development' 'deeply misleading' (Karpinski 2022: 123). Welchman describes accurately 'the standard view . . . that Hegel is primarily responsible for making the nineteenth century the "historical" century, dipping everything, including philosophical thought itself, in the universal solvent of time' and wisely distances his interpretation from such a view (Welchman 2016: 195–196).

system, *only one* dimension of 'absolute being'. 'Originary' being contains *equally* two other dimensions, logos and nature, without which nothing can *be*. Consequently, *historical* time, as something pertaining to spirit, could not determine being's *totality*. Historical time coexists in 'absolute being' with natural ('mathematical') time (the time of nature qua nature) *and a timeless eternity* (the purity of logos qua logos).

It is exactly on this idea of 'the *system*' that early Heidegger's interpretation of Hegel rests. His 'confrontation' with Hegel stems precisely from the fact that he respects this idea.[94] By contrast, Kojève and all those who 'historicize' and 'temporalize' Hegelian philosophy, in the sense that they take history and time to be the ground of Hegel's ontology, do *not* respect Hegel's idea of the system. Instead of taking 'the absolute's' three dimensions to be equally originary, they claim that spirit, which is *only one* of the three dimensions, has a priority over the other two.

## Conclusion

*Heidegger*'s early phenomenology makes Dasein's temporality, which is marked by finitude, the ground of any understanding of being (ontology). This is established through a phenomenological-transcendental analysis of the phenomena constituting Dasein's everyday 'experience', which are presented to it 'at first and for the most part'. This is the 'ontic', 'factical' basis of Heidegger's enquiry into the meaning of being and what makes it specifically 'phenomenological'. For early Heidegger, because philosophy is undertaken by Dasein, which is always already 'thrown' into and hence embedded in a historical 'world', it cannot begin but with the structures constituting such embeddedness.[95] As an author illuminatingly puts it, 'the pretension that thought can extricate itself from [such embeddedness] ... is, for Heidegger, an illusion 'founded' upon non-original conceptions of existence and being. ... Such other-worldly hypotheses ... den[y] perspective, and thus, life itself' (Luchte 2008: 1). This is the illusion pertaining to 'idealist ... ontologies' and contrasts with phenomenology's having 'a desire for the truth of *things themselves*' (Luchte 2008: 1). The idealist 'illusion' that thought can extricate itself from Dasein's being-in-the-world[96] cuts off the link between time and this being

[94] Surber (1979: 367) disagrees with this.

[95] 'The presupposition of philosophy is not an assumption with whose help we tentatively experiment, only to exchange it hastily for some other assumption. Rather, its pre-supposition is the history of the manifestation of beings as a whole, which is already taking place and where we find ourselves already situated' (HPG 53/37).

[96] 'Dasein is that entity which is characterized as *being-in-the-world*. Human life is not some subject that has to perform some trick in order to enter the world' (CT 7).

with the result that the idealists, Hegel in particular, 'interpret' time 'vulgarly' as 'now-time'. Moreover, such a severance of time from Dasein's being-in-the-world leads to the 'dimensionalist' thesis that time is *only one* dimension of ontology, not its absolute ground, allowing thus timelessness to be anointed *another* ontological dimension.

*Hegel*'s idea of how philosophy should begin the enquiry into the meaning of being is the opposite of Heidegger's. He argues in the *Phenomenology* that any attempt to begin philosophy (the enquiry into the meaning of being) with 'natural consciousness', which is the equivalent of Heidegger's Dasein and the structure of a subject embedded in and affected by a spatio-temporal 'world', fails. Any such attempt, Hegel maintains, can never give us anything more than the phenomenal being of natural consciousness: it is always attached to such a consciousness, so that *being as such* never gets disclosed. Hegel would say that it is unsurprising that Heidegger makes temporality (a structure of Dasein) the ground of the understanding of being, for his enquiry *begins* with Dasein. If philosophy begins with Dasein, it cannot but end with Dasein. Yet it is not Dasein that is ontology's 'subject-matter', but, rather, being.[97] In Hegel's view, the only way to disclose the meaning of being undogmatically, without falling prey to assumptions and presuppositions, is to begin with the positing of *pure, indeterminate being.*

Thus, while early Heidegger sees any enquiry into the meaning of being that does not begin with Dasein and its embeddedness in a world as an 'illusion', as beginning away from 'things themselves', Hegel sees any ontological enquiry beginning with human existence and its being-in-the-world (what he calls 'natural consciousness'), as dogmatic and structurally incapable of ever arriving at the meaning of being as such. In this Element, I have not attempted a resolution of this particular issue of Heidegger's early 'confrontation' with Hegel, which is, one might say, the heart of the matter. In other words, I have not answered the question 'who is right?', which is the highest philosophical question pertaining to this dispute (see Pippin 2024: xi–xii and Trisokkas (2024)) and requires a detailed juxtaposition of Heidegger's *phenomenological method* and Hegel's *speculative method* and an adjudication on their merits and demerits. Relating to this is the fact that I have not even attempted to challenge the theses on which Heidegger's *critique* of Hegel rests.

---

97 Contrast Hegel's position with what Heidegger writes on HPG 43–44/31: 'But what does it mean to enter into philosophy? It means that we yield to what is essential in philosophy, so that, in view of the tasks shown there, we may gain clarity *about ourselves*.' Hegel would say that we enter into philosophy so that we may gain clarity about *being* (only *part* of which is the clarity about ourselves).

What I have done is to argue for the general correctness of early Heidegger's *reading* of Hegel and clarify his *critique* of Hegel. Precisely because Hegel begins his ontological enquiry ('the system') with the positing of sheer *being* – that is, with being 'before' it is determined through space and time – he is able to make timelessness ('infinity', 'eternity') a fundamental dimension of 'absolute being'. He is thus 'the last great speculative thinker of the infinite in the continental tradition' (Schmidt 1988: 5). In Hegelian logic, being proves to be 'the concept' or 'the absolute idea', so timelessness proves to be an indispensable dimension of *the concept*. Yet 'timelessness' here means simply *purity*, that which is independent of intuition/matter (nature)[98] and history (spirit). Hegel explains purity through the development of the self-determined logos (the categories of pure thought), but he does not explain it *away* (as a 'bad' 'abstraction'). Being (absolute being, the concept) consists of *three* equiprimordial dimensions: nature (time), spirit (history), and logos (eternity). This Heidegger, *but not Kojève*, affirms in his Hegel interpretation.

Establishing the thesis that eternity is a dimension of absolute being has colossal ramifications for our understanding of Hegel. The traditional and still popular understanding of Hegelian philosophy is that it is 'historicist'.[99] I call a philosophy 'historicist' if it takes history or 'historicity' (and hence time) to be the *sole* ground of the understanding of being.[100] If a philosophy historicizes ontology, then it necessarily temporalizes ontology. As seen, Kojève interprets Hegel in precisely these terms, taking 'the concept' to be identical with 'historical time'. This Element has shown that Kojève is wrong and Heidegger right: Hegelian philosophy is not 'historicist', since eternity is therein a fundamental dimension of ontology[101] and history is therein *another* such dimension. In the Hegelian system, the one does not cancel the other. Yet Heidegger thinks that this 'dimensionalist' idea of Hegel is *false*, since, for him, time covers the whole ground of ontology: it is the *only* horizon in which the meaning of being can be disclosed.

98 Stein (2021: 271) describes the pure concepts of logic as 'immaterial'.

99 According to Williams, what defines Hegelian philosophy is that it historicizes the transcendental (Williams 1985, 1986, 1989: 141).

100 '[For] historicism . . . everything is dissolved into history' (CT 20).

101 Recall that 'history . . . is ruled by divine providence' (Enz III §377 Zusatz/4).

# Abbreviations

## I Works by G. W. F. Hegel

Enz I: *Enzyklopädie der philosophischen Wissenschaften im Grundrisse 1830: Die Wissenschaft der Logik/Encyclopedia of the Philosophical Sciences in Basic Outline: Part I: Science of Logic*

Enz II: *Enzyklopädie der philosophischen Wissenschaften im Grundrisse 1830: Die Naturphilosophie/Hegel's Philosophy of Nature*

Enz III: *Enzyklopädie der philosophischen Wissenschaften im Grundrisse 1830: Die Philosophie des Geistes/Philosophy of Mind*

OHU: How the Ordinary Human Understanding Takes Philosophy (as Displayed in the Works of Mr. Krug)

PG: *Phänomenologie des Geistes/Phenomenology of Spirit*

SL: *The Science of Logic*

VG: *Die Vernunft in der Geschichte: Einleitung in die Philosophie der Weltgeschichte*

WL I: *Wissenschaft der Logik I*

WL II: *Wissenschaft der Logik II*

## II Works by M. Heidegger

BPP: *The Basic Problems of Phenomenology*

CT: *The Concept of Time*

HPG: *Hegels Phänomenologie des Geistes/Hegel's Phenomenology of Spirit*

SZ: *Sein und Zeit/Being and Time*

Logik: *Logik: Die Frage nach der Wahrheit/Logic: The Question of Truth*

# References


Alweiss, L. (2002). Heidegger and 'The Concept of Time'. *History of the Human Sciences* 15(3), 117–132.

Aschenberg, R. (1976). Der Wahrheitsbegriff in Hegels *Phänomenologie des Geistes*. In K. Hartmann, ed., *Die ontologische Option*. Berlin: De Gruyter, pp. 211–308.

Blattner, W. D. (1999). *Heidegger's Temporal Idealism*. Cambridge: Cambridge University Press.

Caputo, J. D. (1977). The Question of Being and Transcendental Phenomenology: Reflections on Heidegger's Relationship to Husserl. *Research in Phenomenology* 7, 84–105.

Caputo, J. D. (1986). Husserl, Heidegger, and the Question of a 'Hermeneutic' Phenomenology. In J. J. Kockelmans, ed., *A Companion to Martin Heidegger's 'Being and Time'*. Washington, DC: University Press of America, pp. 104–126.

Collins, A. B. (2001). Justification and Time in Hegel's *Phenomenology*. *Bulletin of the Hegel Society of Great Britain* 43, 15–42.

De Boer, K. (2000). *Thinking in the Light of Time: Heidegger's Encounter with Hegel*. Albany: State University of New York Press.

Di Giovanni, G. (2010). Introduction. In G. W. F. Hegel, *The Science of Logic*. Trans. G. Di Giovanni. Cambridge: Cambridge University Press, pp. xi–lxxiv.

Gabriel, M. (2021). Heidegger on Hegel on Time. In C. D. Coe, ed., *The Palgrave Handbook of German Idealism and Phenomenology*. Cham: Palgrave Macmillan, pp. 343–359.

Gadamer, H.-G. (1977). *Philosophical Hermeneutics*. Trans. D. Linge. Los Angeles: University of California Press.

Gorner, P. (2007). *Heidegger's* Being and Time. Cambridge: Cambridge University Press.

Harris, H. S. (1997). *Hegel's Ladder*, Vol. I. Indianapolis, IN: Hackett.

Hartmann, N. (1957). Aristoteles und Hegel. In N. Hartmann, *Kleinere Schriften*, Vol. II. Berlin: De Gruyter, pp. 214–251.

Hegel, G. W. F. (1917). *Die Vernunft in der Geschichte: Einleitung in die Philosophie der Weltgeschichte*. Leipzig: Meiner.

Hegel, G. W. F. (1977). *Phenomenology of Spirit*. Trans. A. V. Miller. Oxford: Oxford University Press.

Hegel, G. W. F. (1986). *Enzyklopädie der philosophischen Wissenschaften im Grundrisse 1830: Die Naturphilosophie*. Frankfurt: Suhrkamp.

Hegel, G. W. F. (1986). *Enzyklopädie der philosophischen Wissenschaften im Grundrisse 1830: Die Philosophie des Geistes*. Frankfurt: Suhrkamp.

Hegel, G. W. F. (1986). *Enzyklopädie der philosophischen Wissenschaften im Grundrisse 1830: Die Wissenschaft der Logik*. Frankfurt: Suhrkamp.

Hegel, G. W. F. (1986). *Wissenschaft der Logik I*. Frankfurt: Suhrkamp.

Hegel, G. W. F. (1986). *Wissenschaft der Logik II*. Frankfurt: Suhrkamp.

Hegel, G. W. F. (1989). *Phänomenologie des Geistes*. Frankfurt: Suhrkamp.

Hegel, G. W. F. (2000). How the Ordinary Human Understanding Takes Philosophy (as Displayed in the Works of Mr. Krug). In G. di Giovanni and H. S. Harris, eds., *Between Kant and Hegel: Texts in the Development of Post-Kantian Idealism*. Indianapolis, IN: Hackett, pp. 292–310.

Hegel, G. W. F. (2004). *Hegel's Philosophy of Nature*. Trans. A. V. Miller. Oxford: Oxford University Press.

Hegel, G. W. F. (2007). *Philosophy of Mind*. Trans. W. Wallace, A. V. Miller, and M. Inwood. Oxford: Oxford University Press.

Hegel, G. W. F. (2010a). *Encyclopedia of the Philosophical Sciences in Basic Outline: Part I: Science of Logic*. Trans. K. Brinkmann. Cambridge: Cambridge University Press.

Hegel, G. W. F. (2010b). *The Science of Logic*. Trans. G. di Giovanni. Cambridge: Cambridge University Press.

Heidegger, M. (1962). *Being and Time*. Trans. J. Macquarrie and E. Robinson. Oxford: Blackwell.

Heidegger, M. (1967). *Sein und Zeit*. Tubingen: Max Niemeyer.

Heidegger, M. (1976). *Logik: Die Frage nach der Wahrheit*. GA 21. Frankfurt: Klostermann.

Heidegger, M. (1980). *Hegels Phänomenologie des Geistes*. GA 32. Frankfurt: Klostermann.

Heidegger, M. (1982). *The Basic Problems of Phenomenology*. Trans. A. Hofstadter. Bloomington: Indiana University Press.

Heidegger, M. (1988). *Hegel's Phenomenology of Spirit*. Trans. P. Emad and K. Maly. Bloomington: Indiana University Press.

Heidegger, M. (1992). *The Concept of Time*. Trans. W. McNeill. Oxford: Basil Blackwell.

Heidegger, M. (2010). *Logic: The Question of Truth*. Trans. T. Sheehan. Bloomington: Indiana University Press.

Heinrichs, J. (1974). *Die Logik der 'Phänomenologie des Geistes'*. Bonn: Bouvier.

Hofstadter, A. (1982). Translator's Preface. In M. Heidegger, *The Basic Problems of Phenomenology*. Trans. A. Hofstadter. Bloomington: Indiana University Press, pp. xi–xiii.

Houlgate, S. (2005). *An Introduction to Hegel: Freedom, Truth and History.* Malden, MA: Blackwell.

Houlgate, S. (2006a). *The Opening of Hegel's Logic.* West Lafayette, IN: Purdue University Press.

Houlgate, S. (2006b). Time for Hegel. *Bulletin of the Hegel Society of Great Britain* 27(1–2), 125–132.

Houlgate, S. (2013). *Hegel's Phenomenology of Spirit.* London: Bloomsbury.

Karpinski, A. (2022). Time and Eternity in Hegel. *Journal of the Oxford Graduate Theological Society* 3(1), 122–148.

Kaufmann, R. M., Lyssy, A., and Yeomans, C. (2021). Hegel's Philosophy of Nature: The Expansion of Particularity as the Filling of Space and Time. In S. Stein and J. I. Wretzel, eds., *Hegel's Encyclopedia of the Philosophical Sciences: A Critical Guide.* Cambridge: Cambridge University Press, pp. 109–126.

Kojève, A. (1975). *Hegel: Kommentar zur Phänomenologie des Geistes.* Trans. I. Fetscher and G. Lehmbruch. Frankfurt: Suhrkamp.

Kojève, A. (1980). *Introduction to the Reading of Hegel.* Trans. J. H. Nichols, Jr. Ithaca, NY: Cornell University Press.

Luchte, J. (2008). *Heidegger's Early Philosophy: The Phenomenology of Ecstatic Temporality.* London: Continuum.

Marx, W. (1971). *Heidegger and the Tradition.* Trans. T. Kisiel and M. Greene. Evanston, IL: Northwestern University Press.

Nuzzo, A. (2013). Anthropology, Geist, and the Soul–Body Relation. In D. S. Stern, ed., *Essays on Hegel's Philosophy of Subjective Spirit.* Albany: State University of New York Press, pp. 1–17.

Pippin, R. (1989). *Hegel's Idealism: The Satisfactions of Self-Consciousness.* Cambridge: Cambridge University Press.

Pippin, R. (2024). *The Culmination: Heidegger, German Idealism, and the Fate of Philosophy.* Chicago, IL: University of Chicago Press.

Schmidt, D. J. (1988). *The Ubiquity of the Finite: Hegel, Heidegger, and the Entitlements of Philosophy.* Cambridge, MA: MIT Press.

Stein, S. (2021). Absolute Geist or Self-Loving God? Hegel and Spinoza on Philosophy. In S. Stein and J. I. Wretzel, eds., *Hegel's Encyclopedia of the Philosophical Sciences: A Critical Guide.* Cambridge: Cambridge University Press, pp. 270–293.

Stone, A. (2005). *Petrified Intelligence: Nature in Hegel's Philosophy.* Albany: State University of New York Press.

Surber, J. (1979). Heidegger's Critique of Hegel's Notion of Time. *Philosophy and Phenomenological Research* 39(3), 358–377.

Tazi, D., (2018). Translation and Introduction: Alexandre Koyré's 'Hegel at Jena'. *Continental Philosophy Review* 51, 361–400.

Tegos, M. (2023). The Concept and Time in Alexandre Kojève's Philosophy. PhD thesis. Department of Political Sciences, Aristotelian University of Thessaloniki. Unpublished manuscript. In Greek.

Trisokkas, I. (2012). *Pyrrhonian Scepticism and Hegel's Theory of Judgement*. Leiden: Brill.

Trisokkas, I. (2016). Hegelian Identity. *Journal of the British Society for Phenomenology* 47(2), 98–116.

Trisokkas, I. (2017). Hegel on Scepticism in the Logic of Essence. In J. Kozatsas, G. Faraklas, K. Vieweg, and S. Synegianni, eds., *Hegel and Scepticism*. Berlin: De Gruyter, pp. 99–120.

Trisokkas, I. (2021). Phenomenology as Metaphysics: On Heidegger's Interpretation of Hegel's *Phenomenology of Spirit*. *Symposium: Canadian Journal of Philosophy* 25(2), 125–154.

Trisokkas, I. (2022a). Heidegger on the Beginning of Hegel's Phenomenology. In I. Boldyrev and S. Stein, eds., *Interpreting Hegel's* Phenomenology of Spirit*: Expositions and Critique of Contemporary Readings*. London: Routledge, pp. 14–32.

Trisokkas, I. (2022b). Being, Presence, and Implication in Heidegger's Critique of Hegel. *Hegel Bulletin* 44(2), 345–369.

Trisokkas, I. (2024). Being, Meaning, Mattering. *Hegel Bulletin*. www.cambridge.org/core/journals/hegel-bulletin/article/being-meaning-mattering/A4C60B0F129CC8AC9C22027328475F17.

Trivers, H. (1942). Heidegger's Misinterpretation of Hegel's Views on Spirit and Time. *Philosophy and Phenomenological Research* 3(2), 162–168.

Von der Luft, E. (1989). Commentary on Robert R. Williams' 'Hegel and Heidegger'. In W. Desmond, ed., *Hegel and His Critics*. Albany: State University of New York Press, pp. 158–162.

Welchman, A. (2016). Eternity in Kant and Post-Kantian European Thought. In Y. Melamed, ed., *Eternity: A History*. Oxford: Oxford University Press, pp. 179–225.

Williams, R. R. (1985). Hegel and Transcendental Philosophy. *Journal of Philosophy* 82(11), 596–606.

Williams, R. R. (1986). Hegel's Concept of Geist. In P. G. Stillman, ed., *Hegel's Philosophy of Spirit*. Albany: State University of New York Press, pp. 1–20.

Williams, R. R. (1989). Hegel and Heidegger. In W. Desmond, ed., *Hegel and His Critics*. Albany: State University of New York Press, pp. 135–157.

Winfield, R. D. (2013). *Hegel's Phenomenology of Spirit: A Critical Rethinking in Seventeen Lectures*. Lanham, MD: Rowman & Littlefield.

# Cambridge Elements

# The Philosophy of Georg Wilhelm Friedrich Hegel

---

Sebastian Stein

*Heidelberg University*

Sebastian Stein is a Research Associate at Heidelberg University. He is co-editor of *Hegel's Political Philosophy* (2017), *Hegel and Contemporary Practical Philosophy* (with James Gledhill, 2019) and *Hegel's Encyclopedic System* (2021), and has authored several journal articles and chapters on Aristotle, Kant, post-Kantian idealism and (neo-)naturalism.

Joshua Wretzel

*Pennsylvania State University*

Joshua Wretzel is Assistant Teaching Professor of Philosophy at the Pennsylvania State University. He is the co-editor of *Hegel's Encyclopedic System* and *Hegel's Encyclopedia of the Philosophical Sciences: A Critical Guide* (Cambridge). His articles on Hegel and the German philosophical tradition have appeared in multiple edited collections and peer-reviewed journals, including the *European Journal of Philosophy* and *International Journal for Philosophical Studies*.

---

## About the Series

These Elements provide insights into all aspects of Hegel's thought and its relationship to philosophical currents before, during, and after his time. They offer fresh perspectives on well-established topics in Hegel studies, and in some cases use Hegelian categories to define new research programs and to complement existing discussions.

Cambridge Elements

# The Philosophy of Georg Wilhelm Friedrich Hegel

---

## Elements in the Series

*Hegel and Heidegger on Time*
Ioannis Trisokkas

A full series listing is available at: www.cambridge.org/EPGH

For EU product safety concerns, contact us at Calle de José Abascal, 56–1°, 28003 Madrid, Spain or eugpsr@cambridge.org.

www.ingramcontent.com/pod-product-compliance
Ingram Content Group UK Ltd.
Pitfield, Milton Keynes, MK11 3LW, UK
UKHW022144080726
473066UK00010B/740

* 9 7 8 1 0 0 9 5 8 1 8 5 1 *